"This extremely helpful approach is for anyone facing change—which happens to be just about everyone. Susan Gross is one of the few writers who is truly thinking of how to help create positive change, rather than promoting herself as a management guru."

— Larry Cox, Executive Director, Amnesty International USA, New York, NY

MORE PRAISE FOR Seven Turning Points . . .

"Susan Gross has helped many organizations turn their vision and ideals into operational realities. *Seven Turning Points* is a clear and insightful discussion on the phases of organizational development that will prove invaluable to leaders who are managing change. I will turn to her book again and again."

— Maddy deLone, Executive Director, Innocence Project, New York, NY

"No one knows more than Susan Gross about what makes organizations work—and stumble—at key points in their history and development. The advice and counsel she has provided to hundreds of social change organization is shared here for any reader concerned with making sure that frontline organizations for justice and fairness are strong and effective."

— Gara LaMarche, President and CEO, The Atlantic Philanthropies, New York, NY

"Change is never an easy process in a nonprofit organization, but Susan Gross' *Seven Turning Points* can help leaders see what needs to be done if continued effectiveness is their goal. This book is a must read for all nonprofit executives and funders."

— Anthony D. Romero, Executive Director, American Civil Liberties Union, New York, NY

"What a wonderful book! A practical guide for any organization, funder, or board. Susan Gross establishes a common vocabulary for understanding the challenges of organizational development in any nonprofit."

— Rosanne Haggerty, President, Common Ground, New York, NY

SEVEN TURNING POINTS

SUSAN GROSS

SEVEN TURNING POINTS

Leading through pivotal transitions in organizational life

SUSAN GROSS

Management Assistance Group

www.SevenTurningPoints.com

FIELDSTONE
ALLIANCE

SAINT PAUL
MINNESOTA

Copyright © 2009 Management Assistance Group

Fieldstone Alliance is committed to strengthening the performance of the nonprofit sector. Through the synergy of its consulting, training, publishing, and research and demonstration projects, Fieldstone Alliance provides solutions to issues facing nonprofits, funders, and the communities they serve. Fieldstone Alliance was formerly Wilder Publishing and Wilder Consulting departments of the Amherst H. Wilder Foundation. For information about other Fieldstone Alliance publications, see the last few pages of this book. If you would like more information about Fieldstone Alliance and our services, please contact us at

800-274-6024
www.FieldstoneAlliance.org

Management Assistance Group
The Management Assistance Group (MAG), a 501(c)(3) nonprofit organization, provides individualized, in-depth support to nonprofit groups that are grappling with organizational problems, challenged by change or growth, or striving to become stronger.

Washington Office
Management Assistance Group
1555 Connecticut Ave., NW, 3rd Floor
Washington, DC 20036-1103
Phone (202) 659-1963
Fax (202) 659-3105
E-mail: mag@magmail.org
www.managementassistance.org

Massachusetts Office
Management Assistance Group
Phone (617) 323-4860
Fax (617) 323-4860
E-mail: mag@magmail.org

Manufactured in the United States of America
First printing February 2009

This book was prepared with editorial assistance from Vincent Hyman Editorial Services, West Saint Paul, Minnesota

Designed by Rebecca Andrews

Library of Congress Cataloging-in-Publication Data

Gross, Susan, 1941–
  Seven turning points : leading through pivotal transitions in organizational life / by Susan Gross.
    p. cm.
  ISBN 978-0-940069-73-2 (pbk.) 1. Nonprofit organizations--Management. 2. Organizational change. 3. Organizational effectiveness. I. Title.
  HD62.6.G77 2009
  658.4'063--dc22

                              2008047681

Dedication

To my husband, Steve, on whose shoulders I've always stood.

Contents

Acknowledgments

The experience, insights, and wisdom of many people have contributed to this book: Karl Mathiasen, who cofounded the Management Assistance Group (MAG) with me and was my partner and mentor for twenty years; Inca Mohamed, who succeeded me as executive director of MAG and has taken it to a new level of effectiveness, impact, and staying power; MAG's extraordinary team of consultants—Nancy Franco, Robbie Ross Tisch, Robin Katcher, Mark Leach, Monica Palacio, and Peter Hardie—whose thinking has broadened and enriched my own; the Ford Foundation, whose funding of MAG's five-year capacity-building program for its grantees allowed me to test the ideas in this book with more than one hundred social justice groups; Frank Hatch, Open Society Institute, and the Ford Foundation, whose generous grants financed the writing of this book; Neel Master, who has capably shepherded this book through the editorial and production process; Lori Green and Dottie Betts, whose esprit and administrative help have supported me through the years; my husband, Steve, and two sons, Andy and Matt, who have always been my toughest but most loving critics; and, finally, the hundreds of visionary social justice leaders who have given me the honor and privilege of being at their sides as their remarkable organizations navigated these turning points and became even more powerful, enduring agents of social change. I thank them all from the bottom of my heart.

About the Author

SUSAN GROSS, noted organizational development consultant and author, has spent more than forty years strengthening nonprofit organizations so that their people and programs succeed. She is cofounder of the Management Assistance Group (MAG), an organization that sees building the power of nonprofits as a critical contribution to the creation of a more just and equitable world.

Beginning as a civil rights activist in the early 1960s, Gross has devoted her life to advancing social justice. She has been particularly interested in the ways that advocacy organizations adapt to changing circumstances and new realities. As a consultant, she has helped hundreds of groups adjust to change and growth, build strong structures and management, achieve focus, gain staying power, and increase impact on the issues they care most about. She has worked with a wide array of organizations—from small grassroots groups to major national institutions—and learned much from each as they negotiated these turning points and moved to new levels of effectiveness.

Among the organizations she has assisted are the American Civil Liberties Union, Innocence Project, Achieve Inc., Common Ground, Physicians for Human Rights, NAACP Legal Defense Fund, Economic Policy Institute, Natural Resources Defense Council, Human Rights Watch, National Immigration Forum, and Children's Defense Fund.

About the Management Assistance Group

For more than twenty-seven years, the Management Assistance Group (MAG) has helped social justice organizations develop strong leadership, effective management, robust governance, sound structures, and potent strategies. Providing one-on-one consulting, workshops, management training, and capacity-building programs for groups of related organizations, MAG is proud to play a part in building a vital social justice community, and, in turn, a better future.

MAG produces several free publications and easy-to-use tools for nonprofits, including *Advancing Your Cause Through the People You Manage, Boards Matter,* and *Strategic Planning That Makes a Difference.* To learn more about MAG, and to download free publications and tools, visit www.managementassistance.org.

Preface:
Genesis of the Turning Points Framework

PEOPLE OFTEN ASK ME how I got into the business of strengthening nonprofit organizations. Sometimes I offer them the revisionist version, framing all the jobs I've ever had as an orderly progression toward where I am today. And sometimes I tell them the truth: I'd never intended to have a career in nonprofit management consulting and my journey here has been purely serendipitous.

My first involvement with social justice organizations was as a civil rights activist in the early sixties. After taking a respite from work to be a mom to our two new sons, I reentered the nonprofit world in 1969 to do media work for the nation's first public interest law firm, the Center for Law and Social Policy. That led to my next job, serving as press secretary for the Project on Corporate Responsibility, which organized a major nationwide campaign—"Campaign GM"—to make General Motors (then the world's largest corporation) more responsive to social needs. The compelling arguments, massive media attention, and public pressure that these two organizations were able to generate through their advocacy and public education led to the banning of the pesticide DDT, the first federal regulations protecting the subjects of human medical experimentation, the appointment of the first African American to the board of GM, improvements in the conditions at Coca-Cola's migrant labor camps, the withdrawal of many U.S. corporations from apartheid South Africa, and the automobile industry's first steps toward increasing auto safety and decreasing harmful effects on the environment. The Project on Corporate Responsibility commanded so much notice that President Nixon put it on his infamous Enemies List.

Working in these two organizations gave me my first insights into the special nature, dynamics, and management needs of nonprofits. My next job, conducting a two-year study of what public interest advocacy organizations needed to do to strengthen their organizational muscle and ensure their long-term staying power, intensified my knowledge of nonprofit groups. What's more, publication of the study's findings propelled me overnight into being a recognized expert on the organizational challenges facing activist nonprofits. I took the logical next step of hanging out my own shingle as a consultant on nonprofit organizational issues.

Two years later Karl Mathiasen, a fellow nonprofit management consultant, and I started talking about joining forces. We soon found that we shared the same frustration. Organizations would ask us to help them with a specific problem, such as strengthening their fundraising, but our examination of the organization would reveal a number of related or underlying problems that were preventing fundraising success, such as a vaguely defined, unfocused program or an executive director with misplaced priorities. But because we had not been asked to address these broader issues, organizations resisted our raising them. Karl and I envisioned a new kind of nonprofit management support organization, one that would insist on a broad mandate that allowed us to go beyond the presenting issues, examine the whole organizational system, and tackle the root causes of whatever difficulties or challenges the organization was facing. Thus, in 1981, the Management Assistance Group was born.

We published our first article, "Passages: Organizational Life Cycles," in *Grantsmanship News* in 1982. Inspired by ideas in Larry E. Griener's *Harvard Business Review* article, "Evolution and Revolution as Organizations Grow," "Passages" was the first article to adapt the life-cycles concept to nonprofit organizations. It is still cited today. Over the years, Karl and I revised, fleshed out, and refined the ideas in "Passages," based on our real-life experiences with hundreds of nonprofit organizations.

In 1997, the Ford Foundation asked MAG to develop a five-year capacity-building program for its peace and social justice grantees. As part of that program, we created a half-day workshop called "Managing Change and Growth," which allowed us to explore and test the notion of nonprofit life cycles with the executive directors and senior managers of more than 150 organizations.

The more I did this workshop, the more disenchanted I became with the life-cycles framework. The nonprofit leaders participating in these workshops viewed the life cycles as static. They fixated on figuring out exactly which cycle their organizations were in instead of keeping their eyes on the real ball: figuring out how they needed to adjust the management, structure, and operating style of their organizations to suit the organization's new size, challenges, and level of complexity. They were left in a quandary because their organizations rarely fit neatly into one life cycle; more typically, their organizations had some characteristics of one cycle and some characteristics of another. Participants then obsessed about which cycle was the best match for their organization. The result was they were using the life-cycles framework as a way to label and pigeonhole their organizations rather than as a tool for analyzing and understanding the important changes their organizations needed to make to adapt to altered circumstances.

> Like me, most of these nonprofit leaders got into social justice work not to be organizational managers but to be warriors for social change. Along the way they discovered that to be effective and have real impact on society, they had to build, manage, and sustain strong organizations.

Another problem was that workshop participants saw the life cycles as a linear progression in which organizations moved up the ladder in an orderly fashion, graduating from one life cycle to the next. They were distressed and felt they must be doing something wrong if their organizations were not making steady "upward" progress. Further weakening the framework's usefulness, the life-cycles framework merely described where prototypical organizations were and where they needed to go but failed to spell out in practical, real-life terms what organizations had to do to get there.

I became increasingly convinced that the life-cycle construct was confusing and missorienting nonprofit leaders at least as much as it was enlightening them.

All of this prompted me to rethink the life-cycles approach and develop a new analytical framework that was more fluid, more dynamic, more nuanced, and more true to the realities and vagaries of nonprofit life. Thus, *Seven Turning Points* was born.

Over the last forty years, I have had the good fortune of working with hundreds of nonprofit leaders who have dedicated their lives to building a more just, equitable, and humane society. I have been dazzled by their brilliance and dynamism, awed by their substantive depth and strategic savvy, moved and inspired by their courage, passion, commitment, tenacity, and hard, hard work in the face of often daunting odds.

Like me, most of these nonprofit leaders got into social justice work not to be organizational managers but to be warriors for social change. Along the way they discovered that to be effective and have real impact on society, they had to build, manage, and sustain strong organizations. My hope is that *Seven Turning Points* will ease their way in getting there and will guide, support, and empower them in the process.

Seven Turning Points:

Leading Through Pivotal Transitions in Organizational Life

To remain strong and effective, nonprofit organizations must periodically adjust their leadership, management, structure, governance, and operating style to fit their changed circumstances.

AS NONPROFIT ORGANIZATIONS mature and grow—as their staffs and programs expand, their operations and dynamics become more complex, and the climate they operate in changes and presents new challenges—the leadership, structure, management, and operating norms that worked at one point in their development no longer work at the next. In fact, the management solutions for one phase often turn into the management problems of another. For example, tighter structure can turn into stifling control, decentralization can lead to self-contained, disconnected silos, and consensus management can result in endless meetings and decision-making bottlenecks.

To remain strong and effective, nonprofit organizations cannot hover or stay static. If they are to move to a new level of effectiveness, impact, and staying power, they must periodically adjust their leadership, management, structure, governance, and operating style to fit their changed circumstances. We call the points at which organizations need to reassess and adapt "turning points."

You will know your organization has reached a turning point when the structure, management approach, leadership style, and organizational culture that once worked just fine begin to sow a host of new tensions and problems. These tensions and problems are not anyone's fault. Rather, they are the inevitable results of change and growth. Nor are these separate, unrelated problems that can be addressed one by one. Rather, they are interconnected (often compounding or reinforcing one another to form an interlocking system) and signal that your organization requires broad, systemic adjustment if it's to move to a greater level of effectiveness, impact, and sustainability.

The author's forty years with nonprofit organizations has shown that turning points are most likely to arise at seven predictable times in a group's life.

1. When a loose, family style of operating leads to disorganization and a lack of professionalism or accountability.
2. When the management needs of an organization outstrip its executive director's management skills.

Seven Turning Points

This book names seven predictable turning points that organizations face. It describes the signs and tensions that indicate an organization has reached a specific turning point, the adjustments an organization can make to ease the transition and remain productive, and the counter-tensions it must manage as it adapts. Your organization may face some or all of these turning points at various times. It may repeat them or face several simultaneously. We invite you to turn to the point that most attracts you now, but do read them all and become familiar with their symptoms and solutions. Experience has shown that early recognition and action can ease the adjustments necessary as your organization pivots in a new direction.

Turning Point 1:
Do We Need to Get Organized?   9

A loose, family style of operating leads to disorganization and a lack of professionalism or accountability. The organization needs to develop tighter, more formal structures and systems.

Turning Point 2:
Do We Need Infrastructure?   17

The management needs of an organization outstrip its executive director's management skills. The organization needs to build infrastructure and strengthen management.

Turning Point 3:
Do We Need to Let Go?   27

A founding volunteer board hires its first executive director but finds it hard to delegate and adjust to a less involved role. The organization's board needs to detach itself from day-to-day management and hand over authority to the chief executive.

Turning Point 4:
Do We Need Focus?   37

Opportunistic, unplanned growth results in an absence of focus and priorities and spreads an organization too thin. The organization needs to acquire discipline and focus on a few key areas.

3. When a founding volunteer board hires its first executive director but finds it hard to delegate and adjust to a less involved role.

4. When opportunistic, unplanned growth results in an absence of focus and priorities and spreads an organization too thin.

5. When strong central direction becomes micromanagement, top-down control, and overdependency on the leader.

6. When decentralization goes too far, splitting the organization into autonomous units that have little or no connection, coherence, or coordination.

7. When a longtime, cherished executive director must prepare to step down.

Turning Points—Not a Linear Progression

Nonprofit organizations do not necessarily go through every one of these seven turning points, nor do they always reach these points in the order in which they're listed. While the first three turning points most often occur when organizations are relatively young and small, they sometimes show up in more mature groups. The remaining four turning points usually occur in larger groups that have been around for some time, but can arise earlier. In some cases, organizations must grapple with two or three transitions at the same time. For example, we've seen groups that had to simultaneously move away from an unstructured, family style (*Turning Point 1: Do We Need to Get Organized?*), fill a management vacuum (*Turning Point 2: Do We Need Infrastructure?*), and rein in unfocused growth (*Turning Point 4: Do We Need Focus?*).

A Characteristic Pattern of Problems Signals Need for Change

At each one of these turning points, a distinct pattern or characteristic combination of problems typically emerges. Board members, executive directors, and staff tend to personalize these problems and blame themselves or each other. Being able to recognize these patterns and understand that they're *symptoms* flagging the need for change helps stop the blame game. Instead, board, executive, and staff can see the problems as normal growing pains. Even more important, discerning these patterns allows an organization to make the necessary adjustments before tensions intensify and escalate into full-blown crises.

Turning Points Involve Balancing Creative Tensions

While each of these seven turning points has a distinctly different nature, they all tend to involve many of the same basic challenges. Namely, finding the right balance between:

1. A productive, efficient work environment versus a nurturing, relational work environment.
2. Centralized management versus decentralized management.
3. A systematic operating style versus an informal operating style.
4. A tight, integrated structure versus a loose, mutable structure.
5. Directive decision-making versus collegial decision-making.
6. Well-defined, specialized staff roles versus fluid, adaptable staff roles
7. Strategically planned program development versus opportunistic program development.

8. Institutional teamwork as an organization's standard for reward versus individual entrepreneurialism as a standard for reward.

9. Active, provocative board governance versus supportive, deferential board governance.

10. Complex, highly developed infrastructure and systems versus simple, barebones infrastructure and systems.

11. Explicit, enforced personnel/operating rules versus implicit, flexible personnel/operating rules

At each turning point an organization will find that as a result of its changed circumstances, some of these creative tensions are tilting too heavily in one direction. The figure below helps you to see that the creative tensions exist on a continuum and that they need continual rebalancing as the organization adapts to different situations or adjusts to an altered environment.

Balancing Creative Tensions

productive, efficient	**work environment**	nurturing, relational
centralized	**management**	decentralized
systematic	**operating style**	informal
tight, integrated	**structure**	loose, mutable
directive	**decision-making**	collegial
well-defined, specialized	**staff roles**	fluid, adaptable
strategically planned	**program development**	opportunistic
institutional teamwork	**standard for reward**	individual entrepreneurialism
active, provocative	**governance**	supportive, deferential
complex, highly developed	**infrastructure and systems**	simple, barebones
explicit, enforced	**personnel/operating rules**	implicit, flexible

As organizations adapt and adjust, they continually balance creative tensions. The figure above shows eleven categories of creative tension as continua, with more "structured" characteristics to the left and more "fluid" characteristics to the right. At each turning point an organization will find that as a result of its changed circumstances, some of its creative tensions are tilting too heavily in one direction. Similar figures throughout this book show the most prominent creative tensions at a given turning point and the typical direction the organization needs to move to rebalance itself.

Aspects of Turning Points We'll Examine

In the pages that follow, we will walk you through each of these seven turning points:

▸ First, by describing the mode of operation the organization is currently in and identifying the characteristic set of problems that arise when this structure and management are no longer working

▸ Second, by delineating the main adjustments that need to be made in order for the organization's structure and management to fit its new circumstances

▸ Third, by discussing typical counter-tensions that emerge when making this transition, along with suggestions for how to manage them

Two Important Caveats

Although every characteristic adjustment and tension we cite is based on our real-life experience with hundreds of organizations that have navigated these turning points, the descriptions are composites that lay out what prototypically, but not necessarily, occurs. What's going on in your organization does not have to match every aspect of the description for you to know that it's reached one (or more) of these turning points.

Implicit in the concept of turning points are two assumptions. First, organizations seeking to make a greater difference will grow larger over time. Second, organizations can successfully absorb substantial and even rapid growth if they've planned it well and built a management structure robust enough to support it.

But do organizations have to grow? Some people so treasure the benefits of staying small—the close community, the horizontal structure, the room to be generalists—that they resist growth. Without doubt, growth has its costs, especially in how much the staff can bond with and relate to one another. And growth, if unplanned and undisciplined, can damage an organization's performance by diffusing its resources, overextending its capacities, and overtaxing its infrastructure. But if well-managed and strategically directed, growth has important

How Can Funders Help?

If you are a foundation program officer, individual donor, venture philanthropist, or other funder, you are often in a unique position to observe organizations as they approach a turning point. You can help in two ways. The first is by asking questions that help the organization realize that it is at a pivotal place. The second is by providing resources that support the necessary transitions. Transition can be costly, especially as the organization works to maintain output while rebalancing and reaching for a new level of effectiveness.

The section What Funders Can Do (page 86) will help you better understand your crucial role in each of the seven turning points.

benefits, especially for organizations that are seeking to change government or society in significant ways. The more staff and budget an organization has, the more it can scale up its programs and the greater its effectiveness and impact can be. Moreover, the broader an organization's leadership is and the stronger its institutional foundation, the more staying power it has to persevere in the long process of achieving social change.

Organizations can choose whether to grow or not, depending on how much they think they can gain and how much they're willing to give up.

A Word about Diversity and Inclusiveness

Every turning point presents an organization with the opportunity to take a long, hard look at itself and confront issues that it's been avoiding, ignoring, burying, or pretending don't exist. How culturally diverse an organization is and how well it's managing its diversity are frequently among these issues.

A nonprofit organization's most precious resource is its people; the staff typically represents 80 percent of a nonprofit's budget. The more inclusive an organization is—that is, the more its staff and board are comprised of people with different perspectives, backgrounds, ways of thinking, and views of the world—the richer, keener, and more insightful its planning, decision-making, and priority-setting are. Organizations working on social issues have a particular need and responsibility to include the voices of marginalized communities, like racial and ethnic minorities, because of the impact these organizations' missions have on such groups and because of the integral, valuable role these groups can play in helping to shape and achieve the organizations' goals.

Organizations have to create the conditions in which people from distinctly different backgrounds—class, gender, race, ethnicity, age, religious affiliation, sexual orientation, national identity—feel genuinely included, respected, and valued and can do their best work and realize their full potential. This requires, first of all, an organizational commitment to building a truly inclusive workplace, accompanied by policies and practices that allow an organization to recruit and retain diverse staff. It also requires a competent organizational understanding of (1) what the benefits and challenges of diversity are and how the dynamics of diversity affect organizations and their people and (2) how diversity has to be managed and organizational behavior adjusted to reap the most benefits and overcome the inevitable challenges. While this book will not delve further into these important issues, our resource list will point you to several excellent publications that do.

Which of these seven turning points is your organization at, which has it already navigated, or which might it soon face? If you wish, you can turn now to the turning points that most resonate with you.

When tensions and problems occur in an organization, they may signal that lack of structure and ad hoc styles no longer work. To increase effectiveness, it may be time to move to a more organized, less causal way of operating.

Turning Point 1:
Do We Need to Get Organized?

In their start-up years, most nonprofits have loose, informal management. *Turning Point 1* occurs as the organization discovers that to increase its effectiveness, it must seek greater definition, demarcation, structure, and specialization.

IN THEIR START-UP YEARS, most nonprofit organizations have loose, informal management, minimal structure, and a familial or communal way of operating. Strong, creative, entrepreneurial executive directors, who are usually the founding mothers or fathers, are at the helm.

To lead, these executive directors rely mostly on vision, inspiration, and passion. They don't know how to manage, but they don't need to because the whole staff is highly committed, motivated, and bonded closely by a strong, clear sense of shared mission. Arriving at consensus does not take much effort because the group is so small and congruous. Whatever supervision or feedback the staff gets, which is usually very little, occurs informally and off the cuff in the course of daily interaction with the director.

The atmosphere is homey and sociable and the operating style is collegial. There's lots of day-to-day contact and communication, so it's easy to keep everyone in the know. The entire staff tends to be involved in everything, playing some part in every event, activity, and major decision. There really is no structure, just the executive director at the center and everyone else revolving around him. Staff responsibilities are generally fluid, ad hoc, and loosely defined. Instead of having clearly delineated, specialized roles, staff members tend to be generalists who can play multiple roles. Quite often, roles are built around the unique mix of interests and talents of a particular individual. This can result in odd conglomerations of unrelated duties, such as a staff member who is the researcher, grant proposal writer, computer expert, and media associate all in one.

The board of directors typically consists of friends and acquaintances of the executive director. Their main allegiance is to the director rather than to the organization. They consider the organization "his baby," are content to leave things to him, and mostly play a passive, cheerleading role. They see themselves as "being there if the executive director needs them," but he rarely does because all the leadership and drive come from him.

Nearly everyone, staff and board, is focused on the program. Little attention is paid to organizational matters, such as personnel policies, office systems, and fundraising. But the organization can get away with this because its administrative needs are still quite simple and it can depend on just a few donors.

Signs That Change Is Needed

When the group's staff reaches the pivotal size of six or more, a number of strains and stresses begin to show up. Confusion and conflict emerge over who's responsible for what because of the staff's loosely defined, overlapping roles. Things fall between the cracks because no one is clearly in charge of them or accountable for them.

The executive director has too many people reporting to him, so he can't keep track of their work or give them much of his time. Staff members, especially new staff, complain that they're not getting enough attention or guidance. Longtime staff, who tend to let friendships get in the way of criticizing any low-performing colleagues, suffer in silence as they're forced to pick up loads that others are not carrying.

As programmatic and administrative needs become more demanding and require more specialized skills, the organization finds that it has too many generalists on staff: people who can handle many different tasks but who lack the depth of knowledge and experience to perform any one job at the higher level now necessary. An example of this is the executive assistant who's been functioning as the organization's secretary, office manager, technology person, and bookkeeper but who now does not have the degree of technical skill in those areas that a growing organization requires.

New people can't figure out who does what and why. They ask for job descriptions, only to discover there aren't any. They ask for personnel policies and find that none have ever been put into writing. Vague and flexible policies lead to inconsistent treatment, and so complaints about inequities and playing favorites begin to arise.

There are now too many people to permit everyone to be involved in everything and an informal system of communication can no longer work effectively. People grumble about being left out, about not being informed of important developments, about the right hand not knowing what the left is doing, and about not understanding how or why decisions got made. The staff's sense of closeness and cohesiveness begins to wane, and people have the uneasy feeling that some staff members are part of an inner circle while others are out of the loop.

It becomes harder for the larger, less homogenous staff to reach agreement, so consensus decision-making breaks down. Impatient with the staff's prolonged deliberations and difficulty in reaching closure, the executive director has to continually step in to break the stalemate. Staffers start to complain about the "top-down" decision-making process.

As tensions increase and the once familial spirit fades, the executive director begins to wonder whether he's a flop as a manager or whether he's brought in the wrong people. He can't understand why the newcomers need so much definition and structure when the organization had functioned so well without it.

> As tensions increase and the once familial spirit fades, the executive director begins to wonder whether he's a flop as a manager or whether he's brought in the wrong people.

Turning Point: The Need to Get Organized

These tensions and problems signal that the organization's lack of structure and ad hoc style are no longer working. To increase its effectiveness, the organization must make the transition to a more organized, less casual way of operating. More definition, demarcation, specialization, and standardized systems and policies are now needed.

Adjustments Needed

Define roles and responsibilities.

The organization needs to develop job descriptions that clarify who's accountable for what and define precisely each staff member's roles and responsibilities. Instead of shaping positions around the interests of individuals, it must design positions to fit institutional needs and move away from positions that entail unrelated duties or overlapping roles. Each job should be defined around a set of interrelated tasks so that each staff member has a coherent, fairly specialized area of functioning, such as one person dedicated to fundraising activities and another to bookkeeping and benefits management.

Broaden management structure.

The organization should broaden the management structure so that the entire staff no longer reports to the executive director. This can be achieved either by adding another manager to take over some areas that are now the director's responsibility, or by having one or two senior professionals (for example, an experienced practitioner or an advanced policy analyst) manage junior colleagues. For this to work, the executive director must delineate the degree of responsibility and decision-making authority he is delegating to these lieutenants.

Provide steady supervision and demand accountability.

The organization must introduce more structured supervision, with annual performance reviews and weekly check-in meetings to provide ongoing guidance, direction, and feedback. Managers must hold people accountable and not allow mediocre performance to pass without comment. They should contextualize criticism as providing the employee with an opportunity to grow and make sure that they balance critical feedback with praise and appreciation for what the employee has done well.

Develop systematic communication.

The organization needs to develop more systematic methods of communication, like regular staff meetings. The executive director should invite staff members to suggest items for the meeting agenda, keep a running list of developments the staff would want to know about, share them in a bi-weekly email update, and use internal email both to disseminate information and to gather staff input.

Clarify the decision-making process.

The executive director needs to make the staff understand that everyone can no longer be involved in every decision. However, he must make sure all staff members have a voice in matters affecting them or their work. He should strive to continue to make decisions by consensus, but he must clarify that consensus means a substantial majority, not unanimity. He must also make clear that, at the end of the day, he makes the final decision. At the start of a decision-making discussion, he should straightforwardly tell his staff whether he's open to any outcome, whether he's leaning in one direction, or whether he's already made up his mind. Honestly admitting that he's already arrived at a decision works far better than going through the motions and pretending that the staff's views will affect his choice.

Establish clear, consistently enforced policies.

This is the time to establish written personnel policies so that everyone knows what their holidays and work hours are, what benefits to expect, and how to get clearance to take time off. Equally important, the organization must make sure that these policies are evenly enforced; few things create more staff resentment than rules that are applied to some people but not to others.

Teach the board to monitor finances.

Given how much work the organization has to do at the staff level, now is not the time to pay a great deal of attention to board development. However, there is one area in which the board of directors needs to step up to the plate if it has not already done so. The board must start monitoring the organization's financial health. Board members must understand that, as fiduciaries, they have a legal obligation to review the organization's finances at least quarterly to make sure that its funds are being managed soundly and with integrity. The staff must provide the board with informative, accessible financial reports that compare actual to projected expenditures and income.

Counter-Tensions to Manage

Long-timers rebel against the increased structure.

Veteran staff may have a hard time adjusting to a more structured, formal style of operating. They long for the "good old days" when no one cared about how professional the office looked and everyone came to work in jeans. They complain that the office has become too cold and businesslike. They chafe at following policies, rules, and procedures and charge that the organization is becoming "too bureaucratic." They rail against the "growing hierarchy" and balk at being managed or having anyone inserted between them and the executive director. They resist taking on any management duties themselves but resent it when someone else is given this job. They dislike being confined to more sharply defined or specialized roles. They're unhappy when their individual interests are no longer readily accommodated. Most of all, they still want to be involved in everything, to have some part in every activity and some say in every decision.

These people need a lot of empathy and patience, a little leeway, and plenty of time to adjust. The executive director should make sure these veterans know he values them and understands the difficulties of adapting. He needs to lead them through a group process that validates the parts of the old culture that still work, such as its sociability and solidarity, and identifies the parts that are undercutting achievement of the organization's goals, such as laissez-faire management that tolerates substandard work and bends too much to the desires of individuals. He needs to help these longtime staff members understand that good supervision is supportive, not stifling, and that achievement of the organization's goals means putting its best interests first, even when doing so sacrifices individuality. However, the executive director must also make clear to these longtime staff members that if they want to remain with the organization, they will eventually have to adjust to its new way of operating.

New managers don't know how to manage.

When an organization formalizes, people who have never managed before find themselves thrust—very uncomfortably—into newly created management positions. They usually have no preparation, no training, and limited understanding of what their new responsibilities are or how to effectively carry them out. These new managers may be reluctant to question their former peers, or fear calling them on poor performance. An investment in management training or coaching can save the organization from the tensions, discontent, and turnover caused by inept supervision. Often, the executive director is the first person who needs to enroll in a management class or engage an executive coach.

Generalists lack specialized skills.

It may become painfully apparent that some of the generalists on staff, including some long-timers, simply lack the skills to meet the more complex demands of their jobs. The first resort should be to give them additional training. But sometimes they still can't measure up, and then the organization is forced either to tolerate their substandard performance, shift them to jobs that do match their skills, or if there are no such jobs, ask them to move on. Although letting them go is painful and often creates upheaval and dismay among the rest of the staff, it's usually a better option than keeping them in jobs that they can't do well and in which they feel as though they're stagnating or failing.

Values can get lost while making changes.

In making this transition to greater structure, role delineation, and professionalism, nonprofit organizations, especially those dedicated to social justice and social change, need to take care not to lose qualities and values that they hold dear. While they need to be more specialized, efficient, and productive, they also have to preserve as much collegiality and friendliness as possible. An example of that is having periodic staff lunches or making space in the day for staff members to catch up with one another informally. Although growing organizations need to operate less communally, they also have to work to maintain a caring, cooperative environment in which people are willing to pitch in and help others even though it's not in their job description.

While managers need to make sure that institutional needs and priorities come first, they also have to make some room for individuals to pursue passionate interests and express their creativity. Although managers must enforce well-defined rules and policies consistently and fairly, they also need to be flexible and open to making justifiable exceptions, as long as the reasons for granting these exceptions are explained and understood by the rest of the staff.

Finally, while nonprofit organizations need a decision-making process that permits the executive director to make bold, timely decisions, they have to continue to operate inclusively and set up systems that provide ample opportunities for staff input without getting mired down in time-wasting processes. While these organizations should continue to strive for consensus whenever possible, they ought not to achieve it by watering down decisions to the least common denominator.

Turning Point 1: Do We Need to Get Organized?

Signs that change is needed

- Staff are confused about their roles and duties.
- Tasks and deadlines fall between the cracks.
- The executive director has too many direct reports.
- The staff favors friendship and lets poor performers get by.
- There are too many generalists and not enough specialists.
- Policies are undefined or inconsistently enforced.
- Informal communication no longer keeps staff in the loop.
- Staff closeness and cohesion are waning.
- Consensus decision-making, once easy, is protracted or impossible.
- The familial spirit is fading, and the loss is painful.

Adjustments needed

- Define roles and responsibilities.
- Broaden management structure.
- Provide steady supervision and demand accountability.
- Develop systematic communication.
- Clarify the decision-making process.
- Establish clear, consistently enforced policies.
- Teach the board to monitor finances.

Counter-tensions to manage

- Long-timers rebel against increased structure.
- New managers don't know how to manage.
- Generalists lack specialized skills.
- Values can get lost while making changes.

Rebalancing creative tensions

As shown in the figure below, the primary creative tensions to be rebalanced at this turning point are those related to work environment, management, operating style, structure, decision-making, and personnel/operating rules.

productive, efficient	**work environment**	nurturing, relational
centralized	**management**	decentralized
systematic	**operating style**	informal
tight, integrated	**structure**	loose, mutable
directive	**decision-making**	collegial
explicit, enforced	**personnel/operating rules**	implicit, flexible

An organization's neglect of management and infrastructure can become costly. At this point, it's time to make management and organizational development a higher priority.

Turning Point 2:
Do We Need Infrastructure?

Many nonprofits are headed by an executive director whose overriding interest and experience is the
group's program. *Turning Point 2* occurs when this
management approach can no longer keep up with
the organization's expansion. The organization's values and patterns must shift to make management and
organizational development a much higher priority.

MANY NONPROFITS, especially those working for social change, are
headed by an executive director whose overriding interest is the group's program and whose knowledge, experience, talents, and skills lie mostly in that
area. Not only does this director put all of her time and energy into developing and implementing programs, but she pours most of the organization's
resources—human and financial—into program work as well.

The result is a thriving and growing program with a sorely overtaxed, underdevel-
oped, and understaffed organizational infrastructure. There's no fundraising plan
or operation—instead, all the fundraising is done by the executive director on an
as-needed, hand-to-mouth basis. Typically, she waits as long as she can and then
frantically cranks out funding proposals to every foundation she can think of.

Administrative systems and supports are in short supply. Just a couple of people are expected to cover all the organization's "back office" needs. Financial
accounting and management are rudimentary at best. Bookkeeping is kept as
simple as possible, with all funds—whether restricted or not—lumped together
in one pot. The executive director creates wished-for budgets for grant proposals, but there's no real operating budget that balances realistic assessments of
expected income and projected expenditures. As a result, hope and guesstimates
guide the organization's spending and cash flow.

Because of the executive director's intense interest and strength in program delivery, she usually remains directly in charge of the program staff. But she puts little to no time into managing these people. Instead, she expects everyone to do their jobs on their own, without any "hand-holding," mentoring, or guidance. While she may turn over some supervisory responsibilities to a few senior program staffers, they have so much hands-on work to do themselves that they have no time to give guidance or feedback to others.

As long as infrastructure and supervisory needs remain unsophisticated and modest, the executive director can afford to assign them minimal time, staff, and resources. But as the staff, budget, and activities expand, financial, administrative, fundraising, and management needs grow more complex. The director's single-minded focus on and investment in the program becomes a liability. Problems arise and breakdowns occur that, ironically, end up getting in the way of good program work.

Signs That Change Is Needed

The first difficulties nearly always show up in the financial area. Because no one is tracking donations or monitoring when funding submissions are due, the organization misses deadlines for grant proposals, fails to submit reports to foundations, and forgets to thank or follow up with donors. The books don't regularly balance, restricted funds can't be accounted for, cash-flow problems mount, payday is sometimes postponed, and payroll taxes are sometimes sent late.

On the administrative side, there's not enough staff to stay on top of operational details. The files are a mess, broken office machines remain unfixed for days, and everyone's upset with the inadequate phone system. Staff members complain about the lack of systems and procedures. They don't know what the travel rules are, how to get expenses reimbursed or expenditures approved, or how much leave they've taken or have left. No one has been keeping records.

The staff responsible for administrative and financial matters feels swamped, unsupported, and unappreciated. They grow increasingly disgruntled and disheartened by how little the executive director and the organization value or respect their work.

Staff members on the program side also become more and more frustrated with the short shrift the executive gives to their management needs. They complain that she never meets with them to check in on how they're doing or to help them brainstorm ideas, solve problems, or sort out priorities. They gripe about her vague assignments, unspoken expectations, last-minute interventions, and failure to give them any feedback, good or bad. They grumble that they've been at the organization two or three years but have never gotten a performance review. Newer staff people, in particular, feel as though they've been thrown in to sink or swim and often struggle or even flounder because of the lack of guidance, direction, or support.

Sometimes the executive director realizes that she has neither the skills nor temperament to deal with administrative, financial, and "business" affairs. She delegates these areas to others and hopes to limit her involvement to the most important issues and decisions. But often this fails to work because the director continues to make critical organizational matters her lowest priority, always pushing them aside in favor of program concerns. This leads to chronic delays or bottlenecks, with matters sometimes ignored until they become a crisis.

> All the fundraising is done by the executive director on an as-needed, hand-to-mouth basis. Typically, she waits as long as she can and then frantically cranks out funding proposals to every foundation she can think of.

While staff members may have excused late paychecks in the organization's infancy, they now are far less tolerant of financial uncertainty. They urge the director not to wait until one grant is nearly gone before seeking another. Nonetheless, the executive director continues to neglect fundraising so that she can continue to focus on the program. She can indulge in this pattern as long as the organization is young and able to rely on a handful of loyal donors. But as the organization matures, its early donors demand that the group broaden and diversify its funding base and they begin to cut back on the size of their grants.

Unable to carve out time to identify and cultivate new donors, the executive director struggles just to maintain funding at current levels. To grow the budget, she needs to be able to hire new staff who will either help her raise money or free her to do more fundraising by taking over some other aspect of her management burden. The problem is she can't hire anyone until she expands the budget, but she can't expand the budget until she has more time for fundraising. She finds herself caught in a vicious circle that she can't seem to cut her way out of.

Feeling overworked and overwhelmed, the executive director looks to her board for institution-building help, especially in the area of fundraising. But, because she has paid so little attention to board development, most board members feel detached and uninvolved. They're unwilling to do anything more than come to meetings, provide encouragement, endorse decisions, offer advice—but only when asked—and generally follow the director's lead. The executive director becomes increasingly frustrated by the board's inaction in the areas where she wants help, but she's hesitant to push too hard because she's unwilling to risk the board intruding in areas where she doesn't want them.

Turning Point: The Need for Infrastructure

All of these are signs that the organization's neglect of management and infrastructure has become too costly. This is the point at which it's essential for the executive director to recognize how crucial a solid, stable institutional foundation is to supporting and sustaining the program. She needs to lead the way in shifting the organization's values and changing its patterns of behavior (including her own) to make management and organizational development a much higher priority. Some executive directors see the need for this change on their own. Others require the intervention of supportive staff, a concerned board member, a close funder, or an outside consultant to help them see the light.

Adjustments Needed

Build the components of a well-managed organization.

The organization needs to devote substantially more time, energy, and resources to building the essential components of a well-managed organization:

- ▸ Provide staff members with appropriate supervision, guidance, and support, including giving them annual performance appraisals.
- ▸ Upgrade financial accounting, controls, and management, including establishing more sophisticated budget-development, cash-flow management, and budget-monitoring systems.
- ▸ Produce, at least quarterly, balance sheets and financial reports comparing actual to budgeted income and expenses; then make whatever budget corrections or management adjustments the numbers indicate are necessary.
- ▸ Improve office procedures, technological aids, and administrative systems and increase administrative support.
- ▸ Organize a strong, systematic fundraising operation, including establishing a computerized grants management and donor-tracking system.
- ▸ Develop a more active, contributing board.

Install a leader who is skilled at management.

Sometimes the executive director realizes that she's unwilling or unable to make these changes, that she's strictly an innovative, entrepreneurial program developer who has no interest in or talent for management or organizational maintenance and stabilization. She either needs to move on, perhaps to an organization that's at an earlier formative stage, or she needs to turn over management and institution-building responsibilities—and real authority—to someone else. This can be done by hiring a deputy director of operations, who takes charge of managing the day-to-day functioning of the organization, or it can be done by creating a management team made up of the executive director, a director of finance and administration, a development director, and perhaps a program director if the executive director is unwilling or unable to effectively manage program staff.

Create program subunits.

If the program staff is large and multifaceted, it may be necessary to divide it into subunits that are derived from the functions people perform, such as research or legislative lobbying, or the issue they address, such as clean air or safe drinking water. In deciding how to define these work units, the organization should examine the predominant way it actually plans and carries out its work: Does it revolve around substantive issue expertise or strategic savvy? Or is it a mix of both? However these subunits are defined, each should be managed by a director.

Put in place skilled senior managers.

To make sure the staff is supported and managed well, the executive director needs to create senior management positions and fill them with experienced, skilled supervisors who understand that a key part of their jobs is to foster staff members' professional growth and build staff capacity so that the organization develops a deep, strong bench. In some cases, the executive director may need to go outside the organization to find qualified senior managers whom she trusts, has confidence in, and to whom she'll delegate. The executive director and these lieutenants should become a management team that meets weekly to consider matters that affect the entire organization or that involve significant organizational commitments, risk, or controversy, and to plan and coordinate work that cuts across departments or requires the perspectives or expertise of every manager on the team.

Hold the executive director accountable for sound infrastructure.

Even with strong people managing finances and development, the executive director cannot absolve herself of all responsibility in these two areas. She must still engage heavily in and oversee fundraising by playing a central role in developing fundraising strategy, meeting and building relationships with existing and potential donors, soliciting contributions from individuals, and making sure the grant-proposal pipeline stays full. She has to review monthly financial reports, understand how to analyze them, and initiate corrective action if there's any cause for concern. In summary, the executive director can never forget that she is accountable for the financial health and integrity of the organization, no matter how many development or finance people the organization employs.

Shift the culture to focus on institution building.

The culture of the organization must shift so that the staff and board as well as the executive director place much more value on institution building and management. The staff, in particular, needs to be helped to understand why the new ways of operating are necessary. For example, program staffers have to appreciate why their assistance in developing the substance of grant proposals is essential to the success of the organization's fundraising. The board needs to know why so much more of the budget has to go to management positions. And everyone has to understand that since the job of managers is to get work done through others, it is a largely invisible, productless task. So, although the time managers must put into planning, coordinating, meeting, and reviewing keeps them from generating as much tangible work as other staff, managers are still making an indispensable contribution to achieving the organization's goals.

Encourage an active, critically engaged board.

An involved board, which authentically governs, is essential to building organizational strength, stability, and durability. This is the point at which it's important to deepen the board's sense of ownership and get them more engaged. To do this, the executive director needs to very intentionally shift the way she relates to board members. She must invite them to question and challenge her when they think she's off course, raise important matters with them before she's decided what to do, bring meaty subjects to them for discussion and advice, frame issues in a way that opens rather than closes debate, and otherwise make it clear that she wants them to play a more active role. She also cannot be shy about asking board members for help, like requesting that they help raise money; if she waits for these busy volunteers (with full-time jobs of their own) to take the initiative, she may wait forever. At the same time she has to recognize that unless she genuinely involves board members in shaping the organization's direction, they probably will not feel invested enough to raise funds for it.

If the executive director has been chairing board meetings, preparing board agendas on her own, monopolizing meetings with reports from the staff, or being the sole identifier of potential new board members, she needs to stop doing so now. The board chair must take charge, plan agendas in partnership with the director, and devote meeting time to consideration of governance matters and discussion of meaty issues on which the board's perspective would add value. In addition, a board-nominating committee should be formed, or activated, so that the board takes responsibility for its own composition, in consultation with the executive.

Counter-Tensions to Manage

The staff worries about losing its executive director.

If the executive director decides the most viable course is for her to leave, it's nearly always wrenching for her and the staff. Although they both appreciate that the organization needs a new kind of leader, they worry about losing the director's deep programmatic knowledge, institutional memory, and long list of vital contacts. A thorough debriefing and transfer of relationships by her helps to minimize these losses.

The board wants to hire a polar opposite executive director.

Organizations often make the mistake, in choosing a new executive director, of searching for someone who is the polar opposite of the old director. They insist on hiring a proven administrator and manager, someone who will build the infrastructure and "make the trains run on time." However, they soon find that they're unhappy with the new executive's lack of vision and leadership and weak grasp of the program. Social change groups, in particular, should not let the leadership pendulum swing too far in the administrator direction. Even when they urgently need a director with strong management skills, they should never hire anyone who's not also steeped in the substance of the program, savvy about strategy, and excited about the cause.

Executive and staff slip into old habits.

If the executive director stays in the chief executive role, she and her colleagues must be vigilant about not letting her slip back into old habits. She needs to empower her team of managers to firmly let her know when she fails to delegate enough or continues to relegate organizational matters to the bottom of her to-do list. But the team will need to have patience and accept that her pace of change will be gradual, with two or three steps forward and then one step back.

Funds for infrastructure are difficult to find.

Hiring more experienced and skilled people to handle financial, administrative, development, and management tasks—and equipping them with the necessary support—requires raising funds to cover these added expenses. But it's not easy for nonprofit organizations to find funders who are willing to finance infrastructure needs or provide general operating support. Their best bet is to concentrate on foundations or individuals who have supported the organization from the start and convince these donors that a capacity-building investment will pay off in a stronger program because the program will be supported by a sound and sustainable institutional base and infrastructure.

It's hard for the board to shift its role.

Boards that are used to following the executive's lead often have a hard time stepping up to a more active role. This is the point at which the board needs a healthy injection of new members who will break up the board's homogeneity and shake up its passive operating mode. This will require someone pushing to make it happen: the board chair, a concerned board member, the new executive director, or a board development consultant. The board will need to take the nominating process seriously and no longer automatically reelect board members when their terms are up or act as though there are no terms. Instead, the board (or nominating committee) needs to analyze and define the types of members a stronger board would need, make room for them by giving uninterested current members a graceful way to resign, and tenaciously seek the right people to fill the new slots.

Turning Point 2: Do We Need Infrastructure?

Signs that change is needed

- Financial tracking is in disorder, with numerous missed reports, deadlines, and paydays.
- Administrative systems don't work—files are a mess, necessary systems have not been created, policies are unclear.
- Operations staff feel swamped and unappreciated.
- Program staff members feel that the executive fails to provide guidance or feedback.
- New staff are left to sink or swim on their own.
- The executive *may* sense that the organization's needs have grown beyond her strengths, interests, or both.
- Staff who once overlooked sloppy management have lost patience with it.
- Fundraising is hand-to-mouth.
- The executive needs board help, but the board is under-developed and accustomed to being passive.

Adjustments needed

- Build the components of a well-managed organization: supervision, finance, policies, procedures, development, and governance.
- Install a leader who is skilled at management.
- Create program subunits.
- Put in place skilled senior managers .
- Hold the executive director accountable for sound infrastructure.
- Shift the culture to focus on institution building.
- Encourage an active, critically engaged board.

Counter-tensions to manage

- Staff worry about losing their executive director.
- Board wants to hire a polar opposite executive director.
- Executive and staff slip into old habits.
- Funds for infrastructure are difficult to find.
- It's hard for the board to shift its role.

Rebalancing creative tensions

As shown in the figure below, the primary creative tensions to be rebalanced at this turning point are those related to operating style, structure, governance, infrastructure and systems, and personnel/operating rules.

systematic	**operating style**	informal
tight, integrated	**structure**	loose, mutable
active, provocative	**governance**	supportive, deferential
complex, highly developed	**infrastructure and systems**	simple, barebones
explicit, enforced	**personnel/operating rules**	implicit, flexible

If an organization is to grow, it will need to attract a strong leader. The board must relinquish its high degree of control, shifting to a governance role and handing over day-to-day authority to the executive director.

Turning Point 3:
Do We Need to Let Go?

Organizations that start out being run by volunteers have hands-on boards that function as the staff as well. At *Turning Point 3*, the board sees that its organization is stuck and won't grow beyond its current size or level of activity as long as it relies solely on volunteers. To attract and keep a strong staff, the board has to let go of day-to-day control, shift to a governance role, and hand the executive director both responsibility and authority for running the organization.

SOME NONPROFITS START OUT being run entirely by volunteers. A small group of people, committed to a common cause, band together to create an organization. Often these are membership organizations set up to represent the views and advance the values or interests of the members. The founding volunteers serve as both the board and staff; there is no differentiation between the two roles. The same people who define the mission and goals and design the program also carry out all the activities, write the funding solicitations, stuff the envelopes, make the photocopies, and empty the trash. The office is in someone's basement. The operating style is highly informal and a little willy-nilly. The group's focus is on the immediate; anything more than six months from now is considered long term. Nonetheless, the group manages to get a remarkable amount done because of its zeal for the mission, cooperative can-do spirit, and strong sense of camaraderie. Everyone pitches in and does whatever's necessary, no matter how demanding or mundane, to get the work done and keep the organization going.

Usually there's one person who puts in more time, takes on more jobs, and takes more initiative than anyone else. The others elect him board chair and increasingly depend on him for leadership and coordination. He, in turn, counts on the most active volunteers to serve as point people or committee chairs in each main area of the organization's functioning. The whole board continues to meet frequently and make important decisions collectively, but it's content to let the chair and his inner circle of volunteers make day-to-day decisions on their own.

The organization achieves some success, which whets its appetite for more. It expands a bit but then finds itself at a standstill. New opportunities arise, but the organization is unable to seize them. It can't recruit enough dependable new volunteers, and the initial cadre is stretched to the limit, growing tired, and failing to follow through. The board sees that the organization is stuck at its current size and level of activity and realizes that it will never move beyond this stage as long as it relies solely on the efforts of part-time volunteers. Wanting to have greater impact, the group decides it must become more professional and resolves to hire a full-time staff person and set up a "real" office. An all-out push is made to raise the necessary funds, reach the group's goal, and start the search process.

> The organization is stuck at its current size and level of activity and realizes that it will never move beyond this stage as long as it relies solely on the efforts of part-time volunteers.

Signs That Change Is Needed

Thinking they want someone who will "take over," the board members advertise for an "executive director," and an enterprising professional takes the job. He assumes that "taking over" means leading the organization but soon learns how wrong he is. While the volunteer board members gladly turn over much of the work to him, especially the tasks they no longer want to do, they insist on remaining in charge and making every significant decision. For example, they ask the director to scope out possible office space, but they want to choose its final location. They expect him to keep track of the organization's money, but they want to decide how it should be spent. They charge him with writing grant proposals but dictate what to seek funding for. The board chair and committee chairs, in particular, veer unpredictably between completely stepping out of day-to-day operations and injecting themselves in operating details, like telling the director what font to use in the newsletter, how to arrange the office, or what brand of computer to buy.

From the board members' point of view, they are simply playing the role they've always played. They're proud of having built this organization from nothing and, understandably, see themselves as its rightful owners. They believe that no one "gets" the organization the way they do, that only they know what's best for it, and that no one outside the inner circle can be trusted to keep it on track. They interpret the executive director's attempts to assert leadership as a desire to take the organization away from them and marginalize their role. This makes them even more possessive and more protective of what they consider their prerogatives.

Despite their wariness, board members urge the executive director to make the organization grow and are unaware that they're giving him very mixed signals. On the one hand, they ask him to take more initiative and assume more responsibility. On the other hand, they warn him not to do anything important without first getting their guidance and approval. They demand that he run the program but insist that he do it their way. They allow him to hire a staff assistant but then tell her what to do. They expect him to take on the accountability of an executive director but then require him to function with the acquiescence of a board assistant, getting their sign-off and following their orders.

> The board expects the director to take on the accountability of an executive but then requires him to function with the acquiescence of a board assistant, getting the board's sign-off and following its orders. Frustrated, the director quits.

Frustrated by what he views as the board's micromanaging and convinced that the board's tight control will keep the organization stuck at its present level of development, the first director quits. Often the board makes the same mistake again, hiring a "director," then treating her as a subordinate and driving her to resign. Sometimes the board goes to the opposite extreme and hires someone willing to function as an assistant, only to become dissatisfied with her inability to move the organization beyond where it is. After going through two or three such people, the board realizes that something systemic is not working.

Turning Point: The Need to Let Go

This is the point at which the board has to recognize that if it wants the organization to grow, it will have to attract and keep a strong, enterprising staff leader, and to do that, it will have to make a major shift in the way it relates to the executive director and staff. The board must relinquish its high degree of control, shift to a governance role, and hand the executive director both responsibility and authority for running the organization on a day-to-day basis.

Adjustments Needed

The board must let go of management.

Board members need to stop injecting themselves into management and recognize that, as part-time volunteers, they simply cannot maintain the same comprehensive view and detailed knowledge of operations that the executive director can. Moreover, they must grasp that they will not be able to retain a skilled executive director worthy of their confidence and trust if they keep on micromanaging and interfering in his decisions.

The board must shift to a governance role.

The board needs to understand that its greatest value lies not in immersing itself in operating details, but rather in having a broader, more objective perspective on the organization that enables it to focus on the big picture. Boards that are too involved in management nearly always pay too little attention to their most important role: governance. In this role, the board's main jobs are to articulate the organization's vision and core values, define its mission and goals, set its long-range and strategic direction, determine what its program and organizational priorities should be, approve its budget, monitor its financial health, establish overall policies to govern the conduct of the staff and organization, choose the executive director, hold him accountable, and help raise funds to sustain the organization.

Encourage the executive director to play a role in governance matters.

In making this shift, the board needs to recognize that the executive director has an essential role to play in the board's policy-making and governance decisions. An effective executive director frames issues for board consideration, prepares background information, presents options for the board to weigh, and makes recommendations based on the staff's day-to-day familiarity with the organization's resources and capacities. The board should relate to the executive director as its partner and remember that the staff is far more effective—and enthusiastic—in implementing policy when each has had some role in its formulation.

Retain the board's final say in governance.

At the same time, the executive director must understand that the board has the final say on governance matters, that he's accountable to the board, and that he must respect its fiduciary responsibility. Furthermore, if this is a membership organization, the executive must pay especially close attention to the board because it represents the voice of the members. The executive director must be able to maintain a delicate balance between asserting leadership himself and empowering the board to play a strong governance role.

The board must learn that its only power is as a collective body.

All board members must understand that the only authority they have is as a collective body. The board's power can be exercised only when it speaks with one voice, which reflects the decision of the board as a whole. Board members, acting on their own and outside of what has been mandated by the whole board, have no power over the executive director or staff. They cannot tell the executive director what to do, give instructions or assignments to staff members, or initiate projects on their own. If they could, the executive director would be subject to the whims and orders of multiple bosses.

Add new board members with governance experience.

It's important for the board to add new members at this turning point. Typically, the founding volunteers are a fairly tight, insular group. To enrich the board's decision-making and expand the contributions it can make, the board needs to add people with new skills, a diverse range of backgrounds, and different, fresh points of view. Very often, the board also needs to bring in people with experience in functioning as members of a governance board so they can model this behavior for founding board members and help them to shift from hands-on management to governing. It's also useful for one of these newcomers to take over as board chair.

The new executive director must be a leader.

The board should hire an executive director who has excellent internal management skills, but it must make sure that he is not merely an administrator. He must have the ability to conceptualize programs and strategies, speak forcefully for the organization, give strong leadership to staff, and provide guidance and support to the board in determining the organization's direction, policies, and priorities.

The board must communicate to staff through the executive director.

The board must be careful to channel its communication to any staff through the executive director, unless he has clearly designated a staff member to work directly with a board member or committee. Even then, the staffer must keep the executive director informed. If the director is cut out of the loop, it undercuts his authority and ability to supervise the staff's priorities and performance. If board members feel that a staff member isn't getting the job done, they should communicate their dissatisfaction to the executive director, not criticize the staffer directly or vent their complaints through the gossip mill.

Counter-Tensions to Manage

The distinction between board and staff is blurry.

Problems frequently arise because the line between the board's role of making policy and the staff's role of implementing it isn't clear. The board and executive director soon discover that they have different understandings of where that line should be drawn. One person's concept of policy is another's notion of implementation. One way to begin to resolve this conflict is to turn to the dictionary, which defines *policy* as a definite course or method of action that will guide and determine both present and future decisions. In other words, a decision rises to the level of policy when it establishes principles that shape, set a pattern for, or govern a whole range or series of actions and decisions. For example, the board sets policy when it specifies the overall size of the staff as part of its review and approval of the budget. The executive director then takes action within that policy framework, defining the jobs, hiring the staff, evaluating their performance, and holding them accountable. In truth, the executive director doesn't just implement policy but plays an indispensable role in developing it by making recommendations or presenting options to the board. The best board/chief executive relationship functions as a collaborative partnership, in which each brings perspectives and experiences that enrich and complement the other's so that together they arrive at the wisest decisions.

Confusion occurs when board members act as volunteer staff.

Board-founded organizations usually must continue to rely on volunteers, who often are also board members, to serve as extended staff for quite some time. This is because the staff is still too small to handle all the work and, in certain areas, longtime board members have more operational expertise than anyone on staff. This can lead to misunderstandings and confusion about who is in charge in these areas, the board or the staff. Both the board and staff must appreciate that when a board member is functioning in a staff capacity, she's accountable to the executive director and subject to his supervision. But when the board member is in the boardroom performing governance functions, the accountability runs the other way. For example, if a board member with financial know-how continues to help keep the books, she's doing so under the executive director's direction. However, when the same board member sits on the board reviewing the organization's quarterly financial report, the roles reverse and the board has authority over the executive.

The dual role of board committees adds to the board-staff confusion.

This distinction—between when the board is in authority and when board members are workers or advisors—can be particularly tricky in committee work. Committees play a dual role. On the one hand, it's their job to develop, shape, and refine policy proposals to bring to the full board for review. While the committees can and should consult the appropriate staff when developing policy, the final decision is made by the board. On the other hand, it is the job of committees to provide staff with advice, special expertise, and even hands-on assistance in implementing activities, such as writing a newsletter or putting on a fundraising event. When committee members are wearing this hat, they must work under the direction of the staff, with the staff having the final say-so. For example, in an advocacy organization, the full board, based on the recommendations of the staff and policy committee, should decide what the organization's legislative agenda is. But the strategy for winning adoption of those proposals should be left to the staff, although the staff might well turn back to members of the policy committee for strategic guidance and savvy as well as for on-the-ground help.

Board committees present special challenges in membership organizations.

Committee work causes special challenges in membership organizations. Sometimes committees made up of members (who may or may not also be on the board) must play the primary role in doing some aspect of the organization's work. This occurs when the work is of such consequence to the members, such as drafting ethical standards or defining criteria for membership, that members must play the lead role, with staff supporting and advising. However, when a working committee is operating in an area where the staff, not the members, has the greatest expertise and does the bulk of the work, the roles must switch, with the staff in the lead and the members informing, advising, and, perhaps, helping in implementation. Another challenge for membership organizations is finding the balance between providing generous opportunities for member participation and avoiding elaborate, time-consuming committee processes that slow work or stall in unending debate.

Board members miss their hands-on role.

Some founding board members have a hard time adjusting to a governing role. They miss being hands-on. They experience a sense of loss as tasks they used to do are taken over by the staff. They feel too distant, less central, and less valuable. Some adjust over time and see the relevance and importance of their new role in setting policy. Others disengage, become inactive, and must be eased out. This can be done graciously by setting and adhering to board terms and conducting a thoughtful, selective nomination process instead of automatically reelecting current members or ignoring board elections entirely.

Founding boards fail to assert governing authority.

Some founding boards, in the name of being "democratic" and "nonhierarchical," diminish their authority too much and act as though there is no differentiation between board and staff roles. They invite everyone to sit at the board table and participate equally in decisions. Operating as though the staff has the same right as the board to govern creates confusion, raises undue expectations, and undermines the meaning and importance of the board's unique role.

The board tends to split into inner and outer circles.

Longtime board members sometimes unwittingly serve as barriers to new blood coming in or new board leadership emerging. As the most involved, experienced people on the board, they become the executive committee. They meet frequently, deliberate on every item before it goes to the full board, and bring their "suggested" decisions to the board meeting. The rest of the board feels as though the decisions have already been made and that they're being asked to just go through the motions and rubberstamp them. They feel like outsiders, with control of the board being in the hands of a small circle of insiders who are loath to let anyone new in. This dynamic can be broken by limiting the executive committee's role to making urgent decisions that can't wait for a full board meeting and by putting the newer board members into leadership positions.

The board wants to hire one of its members as the first executive director.

Another snag can develop when the board chair, or someone else in the inner circle, is hired as executive director. This may backfire in a couple of ways. The remaining board members start to wonder why they should continue to donate so much volunteer time and energy, now that someone is being paid to do the work. They cut back, so the increase in paid staff ends up offset by the decrease in volunteer hours. Even more troublesome is when board members discover that the new executive director, although having been a fine board leader, does not really know how to manage or build an organization. Typically, they're unwilling to confront this problem because of their long, close relationships with this person. Sometimes the only way to break this stalemate is to bring on new board members who have no personal attachments, are invested in the institution rather than the individual, and won't hesitate to put organizational needs first.

Turning Point 3: Do We Need to Let Go?

Signs that change is needed

- The board hires its first executive director.
- The board regularly usurps the new executive's authority.
- The board veers unpredictably into operating details.
- The board demands that the new executive run the organization, but insists that he do it their way.
- The board feels possessive and protective of the organization and fears the executive will take it all away from them.
- The new executive quits, complaining of a micromanaging board.
- The cycle may repeat several times before the board recognizes that it is the problem.

Adjustments needed

- The board must let go of management.
- The board must shift to a governance role.
- Encourage the executive director to play a role in governance matters.
- Retain the board's final say in governance.

- The board must learn that its only power is as a collective body.
- The board must add new members with governance experience.
- The new executive director must be a leader.
- The board must communicate to staff through the executive director.

Counter-tensions to manage

- The distinction between board and staff is blurry.
- Confusion occurs when board members act as volunteer staff.
- The dual role of board committees adds to the board-staff confusion.
- Board committees present special challenges in membership organizations.
- Board members miss their hands-on role.
- Founding boards fail to assert governing authority.
- The board tends to split into inner and outer circles.
- The board wants to hire one of its members as the first executive director.

Rebalancing creative tensions

As shown in the figure below, the primary creative tensions to be rebalanced at this turning point are those related to operating style, decision-making, staff roles, and governance.

systematic	**operating style**	informal
directive	**decision-making**	collegial
well-defined, specialized	**staff roles**	fluid, adaptable
active, provocative	**governance***	supportive, deferential

* The board of an organization at *Turning Point 3* has typically been both governing and staffing at least some of the organization. It needs to move from being a task-oriented board to being concerned with the big picture, or governance issues.

If an organization wants to increase its effectiveness, it must stop diffusing its resources, define its core work, and focus its staff and budget in clearly delineated areas.

Turning Point 4:
Do We Need Focus?

Entrepreneurial, opportunistic organizations reluctant to turn down anyone or anything grow rapidly but without any coherence, plan, or strategy. At *Turning Point 4,* the organization discovers it's spread in too many directions. It must stop diffusing its staff and resources, define its focus, target its programs, budget, and staff accordingly, and discipline itself to stick to priorities.

ORGANIZATIONS HIT ANOTHER pivotal point in their development when they begin to have an impact, create buzz, and draw lots of attention. Sometimes their rising visibility is simply the result of top-notch work. Sometimes outside events have pushed their issue to the fore. Sometimes they've filled an important niche that no one else had recognized. And sometimes their leader has become an emerging star and a favorite of the funding community.

Whatever the case, ascending organizations generally share the same characteristics. The group's leader and often its staff are highly entrepreneurial, opportunistic, and freewheeling. They find it hard to say "no" and hate passing up any opening. They define the organization's mission broadly and keep its boundaries loose and fuzzy. This gives the leader and staff lots of room to be creative, seize opportunities, take initiative, and operate with nimbleness and flexibility. Their *modus vivendi* becomes, "Whatever we can raise funds for, we'll do."

These organizations rapidly expand their budgets, staffs, and activities, often doubling or even tripling in size in just a year or two. However, instead of being the product of deliberate, proactive planning, nearly all of this growth is reactive, without strategy, coherence, or overall design. In fact, the only "planning" these organizations do is in response to funding opportunities. Each time they prepare a grant proposal, they engage in ad hoc program development that, more often than not, is done on a crash basis, outside the context of their other programs, and with development staff rather than program staff in the lead.

> A widening circle of stakeholders—board, staff, funders, members, allies, or other constituents—press the organization with requests and demands and push activities they think the organization should get into. Eager to please and reluctant to turn down anyone or anything, the organization takes on more and more.

The more success the organization enjoys, the more opportunities come its way and the more it's pulled in different directions. A widening circle of stakeholders—board, staff, funders, members, allies, or other constituents—press the organization with requests and demands and push activities they think the organization should get into. Eager to please and reluctant to turn down anyone or anything, the organization takes on more and more.

Signs That Change Is Needed

Finally, the organization reaches the point where it is moving in so many divergent directions that it's impossible to discern what its core work is. Staff and resources are stretched to the limits. Some staff members find that when they add up all the projects they're supposed to work on, it amounts to more than 100 percent of their available time. Other staff members think they finally have their jobs under control, only to discover that the executive director has obligated them to some new activity.

Administrative growth does not keep up with program growth, so administrative staff members are drowning in their jobs as well. Everyone feels overworked and overwhelmed and begs the executive director to set some priorities. But she insists that "everything is important." She sees everything the organization is doing as fitting into its broad mandate and being worthwhile.

Staff members respond by setting their own priorities, which means focusing on what they like or on what seems most pressing. Or they try to do it all, giving a little attention to everything but doing nothing thoroughly or well. The organization's work begins to suffer. Its reputation declines as funders and colleagues no longer feel they can count on it for consistent high quality or follow through. Morale sinks. Staff members complain about the organization's short attention span and failure to think in long-range terms. They begin to doubt the value of some of the organization's work. They wonder where its many activities are leading or what they all add up to. They think the organization is diffusing its resources and call for planning to delineate some focus and boundaries for the organization.

At first the executive director resists because she sees planning as closing down options and barring her and the organization from being creative, entrepreneurial, and opportunistic, all of which have been important ingredients of the organization's success. Eventually she relents and agrees to a planning retreat aimed at defining the organization's core work. But the staff (and sometimes board as well) soon discover that there are disparate ideas about the organization's focus and priorities. Everyone agrees that programs must be cut, as long as the programs aren't theirs. Averse to dealing with conflict, they paper over their differences with a mission statement that's so broad and inclusive that nearly anything can fit under it. This failure to set any limits or provide any basis for saying "no" only perpetuates the organization's tendency to overextend. Some staff members start to leave, either because they're burned out or because they've lost confidence in the course the organization is taking.

Turning Point: The Need to Focus

This set of symptoms indicates that if the organization wants to increase its effectiveness and impact, it must stop diffusing its resources, define its most essential, core work, and focus its staff and budget on making a difference in that clearly delineated area. This means redefining who the organization is, where it's going, and what it's all about; redesigning its structure, staffing, and activities within that framework; and developing the discipline to stay focused and stick to priorities.

Adjustments Needed

Push for rigorous strategic planning.

The organization needs to engage in rigorous and comprehensive strategic planning. Sometimes the staff is forceful enough to convince a reluctant and wary executive director to engage in planning, but sometimes it takes intervention by the board. Because the board of directors is not engrossed in day-to-day details, it can maintain a big picture view and readily recognize when there's no coherence to the organization's work and no overarching goals holding its scattered activities together. Board members are ordinarily the first to get wind of outside criticism of the organization. They are in a more powerful position than the staff to demand that the organization defines its core and decides which of its activities are most important and essential. Unlike the staff, board members have more distance and objectivity, are less invested in keeping things the way they are, are not under pressure to take on more than the group can handle, and have a broad perspective that's fixed on the organization's long-term health and impact. Their strong participation in the strategic planning process is therefore often crucial to narrowing the organization's focus and setting realistic priorities.

Strategic planning must cover six critical bases.

To be most effective, the strategic planning process should cover these six bases:

▶ *Clarify mission.* First, affirm or clarify the organization's core purpose, which is the ultimate aim it's working to achieve for society (such as the end of homelessness). The group then identifies its core strategic approach, which is the central methodology it uses to accomplish its purpose and goals (such as influencing government policy). Together, these two elements form the organization's mission.

▶ *Define central long-range goals.* Second, articulate the organization's central long-range goals. These are the major long-term outcomes it intends to produce. Each one will significantly contribute to the fulfillment of its mission. These goals are big and visionary but also within the realm of possibility. The organization will probably encounter some difficulty in defining them because it has been fixated for so long only on the short-term. In choosing its long-term goals, the group has to take care not to fall into the old habit of taking on too much. A rule of thumb is that three central long-range goals should generally be the limit, and if the group adopts more than five, it's biting off a lot more than it can chew.

▶ *Define and prioritize two- to three-year goals and strategies.* Third, define the main goals the organization has to achieve over the next two or three years to move toward its long-range outcomes, and define the main strategies to achieve these goals. Many groups make the mistake here of brainstorming a long list of goals and priorities without taking the critical next step: they must pare down the list to the most critical activities and establish them as priorities. The organization must also eliminate or trim back the less significant work that will spread it too thin. The organization has to recognize that if it is to have impact, it will need to concentrate its staff and resources on a limited number of goals at a scale that can make a difference.

▶ *Establish one-year priorities.* Fourth, distill the three-year plan into one-year priorities, which become the basis for creating departmental and individual annual work plans. (This annual planning should be repeated every year. It should include a brief reexamination of the organization's priority two- to three-year goals and strategies to make sure they're still on target.)

▸ *Strengthen the organization's capacity to carry out the plan.* Fifth, determine whether the organization has the institutional capacity—the staffing, structure, management, financial resources, and board strength—to carry out its program plan. Depending on the needs identified, this assessment can lead to reallocating the budget, consolidating or reorganizing staff units, strengthening the management structure, filling gaps on the staff, expanding and diversifying funding, building the board, or instituting regular annual planning.

▸ *Implement the plan and be accountable for performance.* The final step is to actually implement the plan. The board has to intensify its oversight and hold the executive director accountable for effectively executing the plan, and the executive director and senior managers, in turn, need to honor the plan and turn it into a tool they use to manage and measure staff performance. Otherwise, the plan may just sit in a filing cabinet instead of becoming a living guide that's shaping the work of the organization.

Value institutional focus more than individual entrepreneurialism.

In implementing the plan, the organization must develop a new muscle: the ability to stick to its priorities. This requires a high level of rigor and discipline on the part of the executive director, managers, and staff. Often, this behavior change only occurs if the entire staff goes through a process of (1) discovering the benefits to be gained by aligning around one coherent organizational focus and (2) deliberately shifting the organizational culture to value and reward focusing (because of the greater impact it permits) more than it values and rewards individual entrepreneurialism.

Treat the strategic plan as a rigorous screen, but not as a straitjacket.

The plan should not prohibit the organization from adapting to new developments, taking advantage of new opportunities, or allowing individuals to be creative and generative. However, it should be a screen, forcing the organization to assess whether the new opportunity is more important than its existing work, and, should the organization embrace the new activity, forcing it to decide what to cut or curtail. The organization will know it's gone through a momentous passage and reached a new stage of maturity when, for the first time, it turns down an opportunity to obtain a big restricted grant because it would take the group off on a tangent.

Seek broad program funding.

To strengthen its core programs, the organization has to tenaciously seek broad program support rather than settling for easier-to-get project grants. At this time, it's critical to emphasize attracting individual donors, because they're most likely to provide unrestricted funding. Board participation is essential to the success of this effort. However, board members are unlikely to help raise funds unless they feel that they're playing a valuable role in the organization. Fortunately, few things can deepen a board's sense of engagement, investment, and ownership more effectively than involving its members in strategic planning.

The board may need to intervene in the planning process.

Sometimes, strategic planning bogs down because the staff is so focused on specifics that it can't see the forest for the trees, or staffers are so attached to what they're now doing that they can't see beyond it. This is where the board must step in to help the staff focus and break away from the status quo.

Seek strategic planning or capacity-building grants.

The organization might find some funders, especially those that have invested in the organization in the past, responsive to requests to fund strategic planning. Some longtime funders also may consider making institutional development grants (also called capacity-building grants). In these, the group shares its strategic plan with the funder and asks for funds to build its organizational and programming capacity to carry out the plan. The key to winning such grants is having a compelling strategic plan.

Counter-Tensions to Manage

The organization can't (or won't) make tough calls.

Some organizations have a hard time setting priorities because they hate making the tough choices it entails. The staff knows the organization is overextended but can't agree on what to cut or scale back. Often they simply don't want to face the discomfort of making one of their colleagues unhappy. Sometimes they can't see why one program is more important than another and can't settle on common criteria for making this assessment. Or they disagree about what to keep and what to drop, or they are simply unwilling to close off any potential funding stream.

To help organizations that hate cutting anything, we have designed a way of setting priorities that makes this process easier. The organization sorts its planned activities into three levels of priority: highest, second-tier, and lowest.

▸ *Highest priority.* At the top level are activities that meet all three of the following criteria. The activity (1) is vital to the achievement of at least one of the group's central long-range goals, (2) would make a special contribution or play an important role that no other organization could make or play as well, and (3) has a realistic chance of making progress toward the goal. These become the organization's highest priorities: the work it deems crucial to undertake and on which it focuses its fundraising efforts.

▸ *Second-tier priority.* At the next level of priority are activities that the organization thinks are important to the achievement of one of its central long-range goals but aren't absolutely essential. The group undertakes such an activity when (1) progress is possible, (2) no one else can do the activity as well, and (3) it has or can raise the funding to do this work.

▸ *Lowest priority.* At the lowest level of priority are those activities that would be helpful to the achievement of the group's goals, but (1) some other organization is already doing them well or (2) the chances of making progress are slight.

In all probability, the organization's limited pot of resources will force it to focus almost entirely on the highest-level priorities. It may be able to do some things at the next level if it can raise the necessary funds, but it will almost certainly be spreading itself too thin if any lowest-level priorities sneak onto its agenda.

Freewheeling staff can't adjust to the new culture.

Some staff members, despite having pushed for more focus, can't adjust to operating within well-defined institutional priorities. They feel hemmed in and miss the old days when they could be freewheeling and set their own priorities. Either they come to appreciate that operating with a sharp focus is making the organization more effective, or they realize that they're no longer a good fit for the organization.

The executive director can't adjust.

Sometimes the executive director can't adapt. Her strength is being creative and entrepreneurial, and she has neither the skill nor the temperament to be effective at operating with focus and discipline. Usually it's best for this director to move on and find an organization that needs a leader who can drive rapid growth.

The board is unaccustomed to playing a leading role.

Often the boards of organizations that have undergone rapid, staff-driven expansion have played a rather passive role and are reluctant to step into territory that they'd always considered the staff's. Some boards, recognizing that their broad perspective will add an invaluable dimension to strategic planning, rise to the occasion and become more engaged and active. Other boards can't shift out of their following mode and may need the injection of new blood to prod them into playing a stronger role.

Staff are upset about phased-out work.

Perhaps the most difficult and trying aspect of this transition is eliminating activities that are inconsistent with the strategic direction the organization has chosen. There's no way to avoid upsetting the staff members affected by these changes, and often the loss unsettles their colleagues as well. The management can do several things to reduce the sense of disquiet and disruption. First, the activities should be phased out over a period of several months to a year. This gives staff time to adjust to the changes and allows the organization to fulfill outstanding obligations. Second, the program cuts should be carefully explained to the entire staff so that everyone understands why they were made. Third, wherever possible, the affected staff should be given the chance to assume new jobs in the organization. However, this should be done only when these staff members have the necessary skills and interest. Putting people in jobs they can't handle or feel halfhearted about does them no favor; it's better to have them move on to another organization.

Turning Point 4: Do We Need Focus?

Signs that change is needed

- The organization's numerous, divergent directions obscure its core work.
- Staff and resources are stretched to the limits.
- Staff feel overworked and overwhelmed.
- Administrative growth can't keep up with program growth.
- The executive director won't set priorities and insists that "everything is important."
- Work quality begins to suffer; the organization begins to develop a reputation for inconsistent quality.
- Morale sinks as staff doubt the value of each other's work.
- Staff begin to call for greater boundaries and focus.
- Even after attempting to set focus and priorities, the organization can't cut tangential programs.
- Some staff members leave, due either to burnout or to loss of confidence in the organization.

Adjustments needed

- Push for rigorous strategic planning.
- Strategic planning must cover six critical bases: mission, long-range goals, three-year goals and strategies, one-year priorities, capacity-building, and implementation plans.
- Value institutional focus more than individual entrepreneurialism.
- Treat the strategic plan as a rigorous screen but not a straitjacket.
- Seek broad program funding.
- The board may need to intervene in the planning process.
- Seek strategic planning or capacity-building grants.

Counter-tensions to manage

- The organization can't (or won't) make tough calls.
- Freewheeling staff can't adjust to the new culture.
- The executive director can't adjust.
- The board is unaccustomed to playing a leading role.
- Staff are upset about phased-out work.

Rebalancing creative tensions

As shown in the figure below, the primary creative tensions to be rebalanced at this turning point are those related to management, structure, staff roles, program development, standard for reward, and governance.

centralized	**management**	decentralized
tight, integrated	**structure**	loose, mutable
well-defined, specialized	**staff roles**	fluid, adaptable
strategically planned	**program development**	opportunistic
institutional teamwork	**standard for reward**	individual entrepreneurialism
active, provocative	**governance**	supportive, deferential

When the dominance of an executive director stifles an organization, reaching a new level of impact depends on allowing a whole team of staff leaders to emerge. The organization may also need to decentralize its management.

Turning Point 5:
Do We Need to Decentralize Power?

Many nonprofit organizations are headed by strong leaders who are the center of everything the organization does. Over time, their tight central control stifles talented staff. At *Turning Point 5,* the organization realizes it needs to decentralize power, management, and decision-making, allowing a team of strong staff leaders to emerge and flourish.

MANY NONPROFIT ORGANIZATIONS are headed by strong, dynamic leaders who are the driving force behind every aspect of the organization and stay on top of all it does. For a time, their vision and powerful leadership propel the organization's success and growth.

These controlling executive directors are usually the founders of their organizations. Their intense sense of ownership, certainty, and need to be in charge make them unwilling (or unable) to let go and turn things over to others. They may delegate responsibilities, but they don't relinquish authority. They stay heavily involved in every aspect of the program, even in details, and insist on the final say on all but the most insignificant organizational decisions. The message staff members get is: "You're responsible, but don't take any definitive actions or decisions without first checking with me."

For a time, the staff is not deeply troubled by how tightly the executive director holds the reins. Most of them were attracted to the organization by the director's vision, brilliance, and charisma. They find themselves so dazzled by his mind, so stimulated by his high standards, and learning so much from him that they're willing to put up with his micromanagement.

Signs That Change Is Needed

As the size of the staff and scope of the programs increase, and as staff members become more experienced and proficient at their work, they begin to chafe under the director's close scrutiny and control. They hate being constantly second-guessed. They are frustrated and disempowered by the director's conviction that the only right way to do things is his way. They know that no matter how much effort they put into it, the director will nearly always redo their work. As a result, they stop trying to get things right or make them first rate but instead start handing in first or second drafts. This just reinforces the director's belief that he must have a strong hand in everything if it is to rise to his standards of excellence. Staff members wind up feeling that the executive director has little respect for their judgment, little confidence in their ability, and little regard or appreciation for their work.

Fueling the staff's resentment further is the director's habit of treating the organization as though it's his to do with as he wishes. He makes decisions on his own, without consulting any staff members, even when they are directly affected by his action. Staff members feel that they have no voice in the organization, that their views don't matter, that decisions are just handed down without explanation and without the benefit of other perspectives. In response to staff complaints that he is being top-down and arbitrary, the executive director tries to assuage the desire for more staff participation. He starts having staff meetings at which he appears to be seeking their input, but the staff soon sees that the director's mind is usually made up before he walks in the room and he's merely going through the motions of being inclusive and "democratic." Morale sinks lower, staff frustrations and discontent intensify, and people begin to resign.

> Controlling executive directors are usually the founders of their organizations. Their intense sense of ownership, certainty, and need to be in charge make them unwilling (or unable) to let go and turn things over to others.

Because no work can go out and no decisions can be made without his say-so, it becomes impossible for the director to keep up with all the matters that must cross his desk. He becomes a bottleneck, slowing output and hamstringing productivity. Staff members no longer strive to meet deadlines because they know their work will sit for weeks in the executive director's in-box.

As more and more people become discouraged, disenchanted, or disaffected, staff turnover accelerates. Unfortunately, the first to leave are usually the strongest people, the people who are capable of taking initiative, working independently, and assuming a high level of responsibility, and who therefore are most bothered by the executive director's domineering ways.

Typically, the executive director is as dissatisfied with the staff as they are with him. He grumbles about his enormous, unrelenting workload. He complains bitterly that everyone on staff keeps coming to him and won't take responsibility. As he sees it, he tries to turn things over to others but ends up having to fix their work or worse, completely redo it to his high standards. He feels as though, at the end of the day, it's just easier to do things himself. He wishes he could delegate more, but he can't seem to find people whose knowledge, judgment, and skills are as good as his. What the executive director fails to appreciate is that people don't need to do things exactly as he does in order to get the job effectively done.

This syndrome often becomes a vicious circle of reinforcing behaviors. The more the executive director second-guesses, micromanages, and insists on things being done his way, the less initiative and responsibility the staff assumes. The less responsibility the staff is willing to take on, the less confident the executive director feels about turning things over to them.

> The more the executive director micromanages and insists on things being done his way, the less initiative and responsibility the staff is willing to assume.

The less willing the executive director is to delegate, the more dissatisfied staff members become, and more and more of the strongest people leave. The staff grows weaker, which solidifies the executive director's conviction that he has to stay on top of everything and exercise tight control.

Staff members begin to ask, "Where's the board?" They send confidential emails to board members, asking them to intervene. But, as is nearly always the case in organizations with a powerful executive, the board is used to following the director's lead and has never challenged him or taken action on its own. Members of the board may be sympathetic to the staff's plight but often cannot break out of their passive, deferential role and muster enough strength, cohesion, or resolve to confront the executive director and demand a different style of management.

Turning Point: The Need to Decentralize Power

This organization has reached a point where the dominance and tight control of its executive director is stifling the organization and blocking its maturation and growth. If the organization is to move to a new level of effectiveness and impact, the executive director must let go and allow a whole team of strong staff leaders to emerge and flourish. In addition, the organization needs to decentralize its management and decision-making and shift to a collegial operating style.

Adjustments Needed

Someone must become the catalyst for change.

For this transition to occur, someone needs to be willing to step forward and serve as a catalyst, penetrating the executive director's armor and getting him to see that his authoritarian style is stultifying the organization. This role can be played by staff members, board members, trusted colleagues, friendly funders, or an outside consultant. Whoever this is, their success will depend on how keenly they can make the executive director understand that his vision and goals for the organization will not be realized unless he lets go and allows the organization to operate under a looser, more collaborative style of leadership.

The executive director voluntarily leaves.

Some self-aware executive directors realize that they're unable or unwilling to make this shift but also understand that the organization will never break its dependency on them as long as they stay in the picture. They see that in order for their "baby" to mature and thrive, they will need to leave and allow a new kind of leader to take the helm, someone who delegates, operates collaboratively, and guides and coordinates rather than directs and controls. Typically, the departing executive director looks for a new group to lead, one that is just trying to establish itself and can benefit from his forceful, aggressive leadership style.

The executive director lets go but accepts a redefined role with the organization.

Some strong executive directors are able to let go and turn over responsibility and authority to others while remaining in the organization. Sometimes this is done by redefining the executive director's role so that he's completely removed from day-to-day management and concentrates instead on external matters: serving as chief spokesperson, advocating and expanding support for the cause, developing alliances, raising funds, engaging the board, and building relationships with people who have access, wealth, or influence. Under this arrangement, the director's title is generally changed to "president" and a new person is named executive director.

The executive director delegates to a deputy or management team.

Another way to loosen a dominant executive director's grip on an organization is to add a powerful deputy executive director in charge of all operations and day-to-day affairs. The person chosen must be strong and assertive enough to withstand any incursions on her authority by the executive director. All the departmental and project directors should report directly to the deputy. Alternatively, instead of appointing one deputy, the executive director might empower a team of senior managers to run the organization. In this structure, each member of the team is given clear responsibility and authority to direct and manage a whole department or functional unit, such as program, finance, communications, development, administration, and human resources. When matters arise that must involve or have implications for the entire organization, the team as a whole addresses them, with the executive director breaking the stalemate if the team cannot reach consensus.

Nonprofit organizations, especially those working for a more just government and society, often find the management team approach more compatible with their collaborative values and desire to avoid too much rigid hierarchy. This is especially true when organizations have strong executive directors who, while needing to give up control, still have brilliant, visionary ideas to contribute regarding substance and strategy. Taking such a director too far away from shaping his or her organization's direction and conceptualizing its programs robs these organizations of one of their greatest assets and rubs against the grain.

The executive director focuses on external affairs.

No matter which of these management structures is adopted, the top-level person—whether called president or executive director—assumes the same basic role. He focuses mostly on external relationships and affairs but continues to play a limited internal role. He still exercises leadership in defining the organization's direction, goals, and strategy through an annual planning process and by brainstorming from time to time with the program staff. However, he leaves implementation of the plan as well as management of the staff and budget almost entirely up to the executive director or deputy, taking part only in important, controversial, or high-risk decisions that could have major consequences for the organization or its programs.

Managers must decentralize decision-making and operate collegially.

The people chosen for the new management positions must have a collegial, nondirective management style and a decentralized way of operating. They must become proficient at producing work by effectively managing others rather than by doing the work themselves. Managers must push as many decisions as possible down to the operating units so that the people on the front line who know the work most intimately have as much freedom and autonomy as possible. Nothing produces professional growth more effectively—or develops a new generation of leaders more quickly—than giving staff members increasing challenges and responsibility. Operating in this decentralized way convinces the remaining strong staff to stay, attracts a new group of highly effective, independent people to the organization, encourages them to act on their own initiative, and keeps them motivated and high-performing. This releases the staff's energy and creativity and nearly always results in a burst of productivity and program growth.

The board must become active and involved.

Once it's time for a strong executive director to let go, the formerly acquiescent board must rise to the occasion and start playing a more active, involved role in order to help spark and facilitate this transition. If the executive director knows he's no longer right for the organization but is nonetheless reluctant to leave, the board needs to give him a gentle shove and hasten a smooth departure. If the overbearing executive director refuses to change, the board must play a more forceful role. They may either insist that he delegate power or resign, or engage an outside consultant to assess the situation and recommend the most effective way to decentralize the organization's management structure and style. The board then needs to fill any temporary leadership gap created by the director's resignation, assume responsibility for the search for a new executive director, and reassure funders and other important external stakeholders that the organization is in sure, steady hands. Getting the board up to speed quickly may require bringing in fresh board members and perhaps even a new chair. The board needs members who have no ties to the old executive director but who do have solid experience in performing governance roles.

If the strong executive director remains in the organization, the board's oversight will be crucial to making sure that he does not slip back into old, domineering habits. In fact, it's generally wise for the board to have periodic meetings with the executive and his deputy or management team in order to check up on how their relationship is going and to help iron out any difficulties. If the executive leaves, the board should seek a new leader with the collegial, collaborative style that the organization now needs. They should require this new executive to encourage their active engagement and partnership, welcome their questions, challenges, and disagreements, and help them shift from cheerleading and rubber-stamping to truly stewarding the organization.

Counter-Tensions to Manage

The director won't change and won't leave.

Sometimes an authoritarian executive director can't or won't change his ways, and so closely identifies with the organization and is so deeply invested in and attached to it that he cannot bear leaving. He may go through the motions of hiring a deputy or creating a management team, but he still maintains tight, centralized control over the organization and refuses to delegate any authority. It typically takes a crisis to force this executive director out. For example, most of the senior staff may have to resign in protest, which finally persuades the board that they must intervene and demand the director's resignation. Or a major donor has to threaten to cut off all its funding unless the director moves on and makes way for a new kind of leader.

Staff feel ambivalent about the loss of a dominant leader.

The departure of a dominant executive director sometimes creates ambivalent feelings in the organization, especially if he is its founder. On the one hand, the staff is eager to be out from under his yoke. On the other hand, the staff has grown dependent on his firm leadership, secure in his certainty, and comfortable with the paternalistic responsibility he's taken for the organization. They want him to leave but are anxious about what will happen to the organization without him. This is another situation in which the board can play a useful role, calming the staff and providing them with a sense of stability and continuity.

Expect a rocky adjustment if a dominant leader stays.

If the executive director stays and agrees to shift to a decentralized way of operating, there will be a rocky adjustment period as the executive and his managers negotiate their new relationships. No matter how clearly management roles and responsibilities are defined, it's only by trial and error that the deputy director or management team will discover what the boundaries of their authority are: which decisions they can make on their own and which they must bring to the executive director, when they can operate independently and when they must involve the executive. Inevitably, people will make mistakes and the executive director's first impulse will be to take back the territory. Ongoing clarification, review, and dialogue—as well as the board serving as a watchdog—are essential to getting past this period of halting progress.

Longtime managers can't meet new expectations.

If a new, collaborative executive director takes over, he will expect his team of managers to assume more responsibility and exercise more leadership. But some of the incumbent managers, accustomed to operating with weak authority, can't adjust to playing a stronger role. It soon becomes apparent that these managers do not have the assertiveness, decisiveness, or confidence to rise to higher levels of responsibility. So the organization, once again, must make some difficult and upsetting personnel decisions, finding the right balance between rewarding loyalty and moving people out of jobs they can no longer do well.

Staff are unaccustomed to openness and trust.

Long-tenured staff members may also have become so used to being passive, risk-averse, and hesitant to speak up that they have a hard time breaking out of their cautious, submissive behavior. For example, at his first staff meeting, the new executive director's questions and requests for feedback are met with silence. He must make a pointed effort to change the organizational culture and build an environment of trust. He'll need to encourage staff input, really listen, and respond in a way that fosters more participation. He'll need to show how much he welcomes openness, initiative, and risk-taking by making it safe to make mistakes, by acknowledging that he doesn't have all the answers, by admitting when he's been wrong, and by demonstrating that he can be trusted.

Staff demand too much process and inclusion.

Sometimes, long-tenured staff members swing to the opposite pole. Reacting sharply to the controlling executive director's failure to confer with them, they demand excessive participation. They want every decision to go through a formal, step-by-step staff consultation process involving everyone. The new director must help them recognize that it's not necessary for them to be in the decision-making room for their views to be factored in, because a key job of the department directors who manage them is to gather and convey their input. They also need to understand that prolonged, cumbersome decision-making will prevent the organization from responding nimbly to breaking events.

Some board members won't rise to the challenge.

Some board members are not prepared to take on the greater demands and responsibilities of a governance role. Out of obligation or loyalty, they stay on the board but miss most meetings and do little more than lend their name to the masthead. Rather than tolerate this deadwood, the chair of the board or nominating committee should graciously require these people to either increase their participation or resign (with thanks for their years of service).

Turning Point 5: Do We Need to Decentralize Power?

Signs that change is needed

► Staff, once comfortable with the executive's style, are beginning to chafe under his close scrutiny and control.

► The executive almost always redoes staff work, so they stop trying to do a good job.

► Staff members feel that the executive director has little respect for their work.

► The executive makes decisions without consulting staff members, even those who will be directly affected.

► Staff members feel their views don't matter.

► Strong staff—those most capable of working independently—begin to leave.

► The executive complains that staff members bring every matter to him.

► The executive wishes he could delegate more but feels he can't find people with knowledge, judgment, and skill to match his.

► Board members are passive, deferring to the executive director despite staff complaints about him.

Adjustments needed

► Someone must become the catalyst for change.

► The executive director voluntarily leaves.

► The executive director lets go but accepts a redefined role within the organization.

► The executive director delegates to a deputy or management team.

► The executive director focuses almost exclusively on external affairs.

► Managers must decentralize decision-making and operate collegially.

► The board must become active and involved.

Counter-tensions to manage

► The director won't change and won't leave.

► Staff feel ambivalent about the loss of a dominant leader.

► Expect a rocky adjustment if a dominant leader stays.

► Longtime managers can't meet new expectations.

► Staff are unaccustomed to openness and trust.

► Staff demand too much process and inclusion.

► Some board members won't rise to the challenge.

Rebalancing creative tensions

As shown in the figure below, the primary creative tensions to be rebalanced at this turning point are those related to work environment, management, structure, decision-making, and governance.

productive, efficient	**work environment**	nurturing, relational
centralized	**management**	decentralized
tight, integrated	**structure**	loose, mutable
directive	**decision-making**	collegial
active, provocative	**governance**	supportive, deferential

When decentralization has gone to an extreme, an organization may need to rediscover its core and integrate its programs and operations. The balance of power may also need to be adjusted so staff can be held accountable.

Turning Point 6:
Do We Need to Recapture Our Core?

> As large, mature organizations grow, they often disintegrate into numerous autonomous projects. *Turning Point 6* occurs as the organization realizes that it has splintered into disconnected silos. It needs to rediscover its core goals, consolidate and integrate its programs, and tighten its structure and management.

AS DECENTRALIZED organizations grow, centrifugal forces drive their expansion outward, and they often proliferate into numerous strong, independent projects. This usually happens in large organizations that have been around for quite some time. Four forces keep pushing the organization toward greater and greater decentralization.

First, big staffs must be organized into viably-sized work units. Often the easiest way to structure a growing program is to create a separate project for each new activity. As the number of staff and projects expand, the organization becomes a conglomeration of self-contained silos. Staff members identify more with their particular project than with the organization as a whole. They focus solely on their own individual jobs and projects and care only about organizational matters involving their project's interests.

Second, the organization's decentralized structure and management style shifts most power to projects and weakens the authority of the executive director. She is left with little ability to impose central coordination or direction, define boundaries, or hold project staff accountable. Over time, this allows the projects to function with increasing autonomy. If a project can raise its own funds (as it's usually expected to), it's free to hire its own staff, design its own structure and management, and set its own course. The stronger the projects become, the less possible it is for the director to exercise any central leadership or impose any accountability.

Third, funders of a large, mature organization are ordinarily reluctant to provide it with anything but restricted support. The organization normally takes the path of least resistance by seeking only project funding. As a result, each new grant either strengthens the independence of an existing project or generates a new project with its own director, staff, and distinct identity. This makes it increasingly hard for funders to discern any overall focus, common goals, or coherent strategy that's shaping the organization's work and tying all its projects together. The funders are therefore unwilling to give anything but project grants, which only deepens the organization's "projectitis" and makes funders unwitting accomplices in perpetuating the organization's balkanization.

> As a decentralized organization grows, centrifugal forces drive the organization's expansion outward, and it proliferates into numerous strong, independent projects.

Fourth, usually the easiest, simplest way for the organization to keep track of both its income and expenditures is to set up a separate account for each project. This bookkeeping system ends up reinforcing the organization's fragmentation and tends to lock in its silo structure.

Signs That Change Is Needed

Unlike the opportunistic organization described in *Turning Point 4: Do We Need Focus?* this organization is not merely unfocused; it's splintered into numerous disjointed projects that know little to nothing about each other's work and function with virtual sovereignty. The staff can't see any cohesion in the organization's work or any shared goals. Instead, they feel as though the group is a collection of independent projects that happen to be operating under the same broad organizational umbrella. In fact, that's just what it has become.

Over time, the projects develop into little fiefdoms, each protecting its own turf and vying with each other for funding and for the attention and support of the organization's central "service" departments (such as development, finance, and administration). Because these service departments have no institutional priorities to guide them, they arbitrarily choose where to focus their resources. The organizational culture becomes competitive, territorial, and sometimes even backbiting. There is little to no cooperation, coordination, or even communication across project lines.

People feel increasingly atomized and isolated. They may still be able to recite the organization's written mission statement, but it's a litany they repeat without heart or clear common meaning. They miss having a sense of shared purpose and connectedness and are disheartened by the lack of coherence and unity in the organization. They fail to see any way in which their various projects fit together or add up to a larger whole. They complain about the absence of coordination and integration, the lack of team building, and the failure of one hand to know what the other is doing. At the same time, staff members remain invested in their own project and fiercely protect its interests.

The quality of work becomes uneven, with some projects performing excellently and others not very well. Embarrassing inconsistencies appear in the organization's policies, positions, and messages as one project takes a stand that is quite different from another's. These problems occur because, absent of strong central management, there are no across-the-board performance standards, no consistent quality control, no crosscutting coordination, little to no organization-wide policy or priority setting, and almost no ability to hold powerful project directors to account.

Frequently the board is fragmented and parochial as well. Each board member has his or her own pet projects and becomes an advocate for them. Project directors bypass the executive director and go directly to their ally on the board to lobby for what they want. The board focuses on the trees rather than the forest, and no one in the organization is thinking about the organization's broad goals or long-term vision.

People outside the organization only know the projects, not the organization as a whole, and may assume that they're freestanding organizations. The organization's identity is virtually eclipsed by its projects so that it has no image or brand of its own. Winning media coverage or unrestricted funding that covers the entire organization becomes nearly impossible.

Turning Point: The Need to Recapture the Core

These symptoms signal that the organization has taken decentralization to an extreme and now needs to rediscover its essence and core—the overarching goals toward which all its work will aim—and then consolidate, integrate, and focus its programs and operations accordingly. The organization must also adjust the balance of power so that the staff can be held accountable and the organization can be kept focused and on track.

Adjustments Needed

Define the organization's core work through strategic planning.

This is the point at which comprehensive strategic planning is once again essential. (See *Turning Point 4: Do We Need Focus?* for information on strategic planning.) Most important, the organization must revisit and recapture its fundamental mission and singular identity. Then it must define its overall long-range goals within that context and nail down its shorter-range priorities. This requires answering four key questions:

1. What should be the organization's core purpose, core values, and core strategic approach?
2. What central long-range goals should the entire organization work to achieve?
3. Which of its current activities are on course and which are irrelevant or tangential?
4. What should be the organization's focus and priorities over the next few years?

The chosen focus should drive restructuring.

The answers to these questions provide the organization with a rationale and framework for rethinking the composition and organization of its staff and for deciding how to combine and consolidate its activities, redesign its structure, reformulate its management, and shift its culture and operating style. This normally entails making the following changes.

Strengthen core programs and eliminate tangential ones.

The organization must define its core work and make sure that a sufficient number of strong, well-qualified staff and ample budgetary resources are assigned to these top-priority activities. The organization should then phase out or spin off projects that are not important to accomplishing the organization's central long-range goals. It should reduce the number of remaining projects by integrating, consolidating, and reorganizing their activities into larger, coherent, well-focused program departments, each headed by a director.

Hire a firm but collaborative leader.

In all probability, the executive director who presided over the fragmented, balkanized organization is not the right person to lead the organization through refocusing and consolidation. Her management style—operating by consensus, taking a hands-off approach, trying to make everyone happy, compromising, or giving in to avoid conflict—made her a good fit for the decentralized organization but can't provide the organization with the unifying leadership it requires. The organization now needs an executive director who knows when she should delegate fully, operate collegially, nurture staff, and use a light touch, and when she must assert leadership, make tough or unpopular choices, demand excellence and results, and hold people strictly to account.

In some cases, the incumbent executive director recognizes that the organization needs a new kind of leader and voluntarily resigns. In other cases, the board has to take action, either asking the director to step down or retaining an organizational development consultant to identify what the organization needs in order to move to the next level of effectiveness, sustainability, and impact.

Strengthen central "service" departments.

In addition to trimming and integrating program activities, the organization must build strong, central support departments that provide vital services to the rest of the organization. These departments are typically development, finance, administration, human resources, technology, and communications, but may also include research, field outreach, litigation, and legislative work. It's essential for the organization to establish clear program priorities so that these "service" departments know how to allocate their time, resources, and effort among the other departments.

Vest sufficient power in the executive director.

The new executive director must be vested with substantial authority over all the department directors. She needs authority to provide leadership and direction, maintain high performance standards, exercise quality control, ensure consistent messages and policy positions, establish institutional priorities, manage allocation of resources accordingly, and sign off on important or sensitive strategic, substantive, or institutional decisions.

Install strong deputies to share in central management.

It's usually impossible for only one top executive to effectively manage all these department directors on her own; the span of responsibility is just too great. The new executive director needs at least one other top-level manager to whom she can shift some of the management burden. This could be either a program director, who manages and coordinates all the program departments, or a chief operating officer, who manages most or all of the service departments. Alternatively, it could be two deputy directors, one for operations and one for programming. The latter two arrangements free the executive director to play a more robust external role: fundraising, promoting, speaking, advocating, and building alliances and relationships, as well as overseeing the organization's performance and guiding its overall programmatic and strategic direction. Which arrangement works best depends on the size of the organization; the scope, complexity, and interrelatedness of its activities; and the strengths and weaknesses of the executive director.

Create a senior management team.

The executive director must institute several new management mechanisms that provide for central leadership, channels for communication, and integration and coordination of work. To begin with, she has to create a senior management team, made up of her top-level deputies and the directors of all the departments. The team should meet regularly to address matters that affect the entire institution or require central planning and coordination. This includes setting policies that have an impact on the whole organization (such as changing personnel policies or revising salary scales); making decisions that have important financial or political implications (such as buying a building or developing an e-activist base on the Internet); taking actions that will require new funding or reallocation of existing resources (such as moving into state policy work or expanding the communications department); and launching cross-cutting initiatives that involve several departments, such as campaigns.

Create teams that cut across departments.

The term for the method that enables staff from several departments to collaborate on the same initiative is *matrix management*. This approach calls for the creation of an ad hoc, interdisciplinary team, made up of point people from each participating department. This team plans, coordinates, and integrates work on the joint initiative so that all the activities mesh and all are aimed at the same overarching goals, shaped by an integrated strategy, and implemented in a coordinated manner. In matrix management, each team has a leader who is responsible for convening the team, coordinating its work, and keeping track of whether each team member is getting his or her part done. While the team's job is to define *what* the staff members assigned to the initiative should be doing, it remains the job of their regular departmental supervisors to monitor and evaluate *how* they are carrying out those responsibilities. If the team leader takes issue with someone's performance or timeliness, he should ask that person's supervisor to take corrective action.

Create an integrated, institution-wide planning process.

The organization also needs to institute an annual institution-wide planning and budgeting process. The process should start with each department having a meeting to discuss what they think the organization's top priorities for the year should be. Informed by those views, the senior management team should meet to reach agreement on a set of institutional priorities that will guide the planning of the whole organization. Each department should then meet to develop their departmental plan within that overall framework and identify their top priorities. The senior management team should meet again to review the plans, decide (on the basis of likely projected income) what to include and what to cut, and determine (based on the priorities) how the budget should be allocated.

Department directors must serve as communications channels between staff and top management.

A critical responsibility of department directors is to serve as the communications link between staff and the senior management team. Each director must channel information both up and down. Through the use of regular departmental meetings, directors should keep their staff informed about significant developments or senior management decisions and assemble the views of staff so that their input is factored into the senior management's deliberations.

Build departmental subunits as needed.

Some of the departments may be too large for one director to manage alone. They need to be organized into reasonably sized, functionally coherent, or substantively focused subunits, each one led by a middle manager. For example, a finance and administration department might have three subunits devoted, respectively, to finance, office management, and human resources.

Retain decentralized decision-making as much as possible.

To make sure that the organization does not shift too far and become overly centralized, all the senior managers need to push down to the operating units as much authority and responsibility as possible. Frontline staff should be empowered to make day-to-day decisions about their work as long as those decisions are consistent with the organization's plans, policies, and priorities and do not affect other parts of the organization. Managers should create a collegial work environment in which strong people can take initiative and be independent and creative, but in which it's clear that the larger interests and needs of the institution must always come first.

Intentionally shift to a cohesive, collaborative culture.

Consolidation eliminates the structural fragmentation, but it alone can't change the parochial, territorial culture. Managers and staff must deliberately shift the culture from competitive to collaborative and switch their orientation—and the way they identify—from "their project" to the organization as a whole. Engaging the staff in strategic planning is a good way to foster this culture change. An effective process leaves the staff inspired by a common vision, mission, and over-arching goals, and bonded in the knowledge that staff members will have to think and operate as a unified team to make the plan a reality. Team-building exercises are also helpful. In addition, all managers must be sure to model collaborative, cooperative behavior.

Engage the board in strategic planning.

It's crucial for the board of directors to participate in strategic planning. Their diverse perspectives are essential. More important, they will emerge with a deeper sense of commitment and buy-in if they help to shape the organization's redefined mission, long-range goals, strategy, and priorities. As part of the planning process, the board needs to reassess its composition to make sure it has the skills, expertise, connections, and diversity that the organization and its new direction now require. The board also needs to make certain that its members are committed to the organization's overall vision, not just to one or two of its constituent programs. The board chair (or chair of the board-development committee) may need to talk with each member to see whether he or she is enthused about the new direction or whether this would be a good time to move on.

Counter-Tensions to Manage

The organization restructures without refocusing.

Some organizations make the mistake of thinking that they can cure their fragmentation simply by reorganizing. They plunge into an attempt to redesign their organizational chart only to find that, because they have not rethought the mission, goals, and priorities of the organization, they have no framework and no rationale on which to base new structure. These groups must start over and not skip the essential first step of redefining their core and strategy through rigorous strategic planning.

Tensions arise over cutting projects.

The organization that's recapturing its core after fragmentation usually runs into some of the same snags encountered by the organization that's moving away from being spread too thin: difficulty in making tough decisions and setting priorities, dealing with the fallout from eliminating projects or activities, helping some people to leave the organization, and calming the unsettled staff. It has to manage these snags in much the same way the overextended organization addressed them. (See *Turning Point 4: Do We Need Focus?*)

Lone rangers can't adjust.

Some long-tenured staff members, especially former project directors, are likely to fail to adjust to the new norms and operating style. They hate process, have no patience for collaboration, resent or ignore rules, and prefer to function as lone rangers. These people nearly always have to leave.

The organization lacks the funding it needs to make the shift.

Sometimes an organization is thwarted in its attempt to navigate this turning point by a lack of funding. It takes a good deal of money (as well as staff time that must be paid for) to conduct a strategic planning process, redesign the structure, build up the core program staff and the central service departments, strengthen top-level management, add a middle-management tier, develop a new annual planning and budgeting process, institute other new management mechanisms, and free staff to spend more time planning, coordinating, and integrating cross-cutting work. Once again, a healthy injection of general capacity-building funds is crucial. The organization must develop a compelling case that restructuring and refocusing will significantly increase its performance, influence, and staying power. Then it must invite longtime donors to invest in this vital organizational development.

The organization hesitates to plan before the new executive director starts.

A dilemma some organizations face is deciding when to conduct strategic planning. Should they do it before or after the incumbent executive director steps down? Should they wait until a new director is chosen and installed, or should they have a plan to inform the executive search process? Usually the best course is for the organization to at least recapture its overall mission and fundamental identity before the board searches for a new executive director. This helps board members define the skills, qualities, and strengths the new director must have and enables them to assess whether candidates are committed to the organization's vision and fundamental aims. But the planning does not need to be completed before the new director comes on. The organization should only complete the first stage of the strategic planning process—defining the organization's core purpose, strategic approach, and perhaps its central long-range goals—before the search begins. It can then wait for the new executive director to play a leading part in the rest of the planning and restructuring. If the departing executive director is willing and able, she can lead the first stage of the planning before leaving. If not, a board-staff strategic planning committee can design and facilitate the process, perhaps with the assistance of an outside consultant.

Turning Point 6: Do We Need to Recapture Our Core?

Signs that change is needed

- The organization has splintered into autonomous programs and projects.
- Staff in one program know little about the activities of staff in another program.
- Projects operate as separate fiefdoms; if a program manager can raise funds to do a project, it's hers to do.
- Programs compete with each other for operational services and for grants.
- People feel isolated, lack a sense of shared purpose, and can't see how the various projects contribute to a unified mission.
- The organization lacks cross-department quality standards, and work is uneven across the organization.
- The board is fragmented and parochial; board members have their own pet projects.
- Project directors bypass the executive and go straight to the board.
- People outside the organization know it only by its projects.
- The organization has no overarching identity.

Adjustments needed

- Define the organization's core work through strategic planning.
- The chosen focus should drive restructuring.
- Strengthen core programs and eliminate tangential ones.
- Hire a firm but collaborative leader.
- Strengthen central "service" departments.
- Vest sufficient power in the executive director.
- Install strong deputies to share in central management.
- Create a senior management team.
- Create teams that cut across departments.
- Create an integrated, institution-wide planning process.
- Department directors must serve as communications channels between staff and top management.
- Build departmental subunits as needed.
- Retain decentralized decision-making as much as possible.
- Intentionally shift to a cohesive, collaborative culture.
- Engage the board in strategic planning.

Counter-tensions to manage

- The organization restructures without refocusing.
- Tensions arise over cutting projects.
- Lone rangers can't adjust.
- The organization lacks the funding it needs to make the shift.
- The organization hesitates to plan before the new executive director starts.

Rebalancing creative tensions

As shown in the figure below, the primary creative tensions to be rebalanced at this turning point are those related to management, structure, decision-making, program development, standard for reward, governance, and infrastructure and systems.

centralized	management	decentralized
tight, integrated	structure	loose, mutable
directive	decision-making	collegial
strategically planned	program development	opportunistic
institutional teamwork	standard for reward	individual entrepreneurialism
active, provocative	governance	supportive, deferential
complex, highly developed	infrastructure and systems	simple, barebones

To avoid a crisis, an organization should start preparing a few years before a strong executive director departs. Succession should be a deliberate and orderly process.

Turning Point 7:
How Do We Move On?

In many nonprofit organizations, the board and staff can't imagine how the organization could exist without its cherished, long-term executive director. At *Turning Point 7*, the organization realizes it must prepare for the executive's eventual departure by building the bench strength of the organization so that it's no longer dependent on any one person but has a strong, multifaceted leadership team on whom it can rely.

MANY NONPROFIT organizations have been run for years—even decades—by the same executive director. Quite often, he's been there since its founding and is the only chief executive the organization has ever known. Though he has his weak points, the organization has learned how to get around them and, all in all, he's a highly effective, admired, and cherished leader, and the organization is strong and successful.

Signs That Change Is Needed

As the years go by, the organization becomes increasingly executive director-centric. The board and staff can't imagine the organization without him and wonder whether anyone will ever be able to fill his shoes. He continues to be the lead visionary, strategist, spokesperson, and fundraiser. In fact, so much of the organization revolves around him that the board and staff harbor doubts and concerns about whether the organization could withstand his departure. As a result, they avoid the subject, act as though the executive director will never leave, and hope that they won't have to confront the question for a very long time.

As more time goes by, the need for a succession plan begins to cross people's minds, but no one wants to put the issue squarely on the table. The board and senior staff, reluctant to do anything that might hasten the director's leaving, don't raise the issue. The director himself, though growing a little tired, is so attached to the organization and his role that he's unwilling and unable to confront the question of succession. He also worries about the damage his exiting may cause to the organization he loves.

> The director, though growing a little tired, is so attached to the organization and his role that he's unwilling to confront the question of succession. He also worries about the damage his exiting may cause to the organization he loves.

The more the organization continues to rely heavily on the director's leadership, the less likely it is to come to grips with the possibility of his departure. The organization just keeps blithely rolling along, acting as though the executive director will never leave.

But one day it becomes clear that the executive director will have to step down, either because he's sick or burned out and can't work anymore, or because he wants to work less or completely retire. Unprepared, the organization panics and is thrown into disarray.

Turning Point: The Need to Move On

If the organization is to avoid this crisis, it must realize that the turning point has been reached, not when the executive director departs, but a few years before, when the organization has time to prepare for his inevitable departure. In many ways, succession is more aptly described as a process rather than a plan: a deliberate and orderly process of building the bench strength of the organization so that it's no longer dependent on any one person but has a strong, multifaceted leadership team on whom it can rely.

Adjustments Needed

Prepare for succession through an orderly succession process.

The organization should not take a cookie-cutter approach to succession but instead design a plan and process that is tailored to fit its unique circumstances, needs, and dynamics. The following are the most important elements of the process.

Build a broad base of leadership.

Well before he's ready to step down, the executive director must make sure the organization is well-prepared for his eventual departure. If he drags his feet and fails to get into action, the board must push him to do so. He needs to start by systematically building a broad base of leadership in the organization that is designed to minimize or break the organization's dependence on him. He should work first on the staff, making sure a strong management team is in place that is made up of highly effective managers, including a well-qualified director for every program and service department. He ought to invest heavily in these people, offering them executive coaching and training opportunities and mentoring them himself to strengthen their management skills and develop their leadership to the point where the team can run the organization without him.

The new director doesn't have to be homegrown.

In some organizations, one of these senior managers is a likely or even obvious successor to the reigning executive director. In other organizations, there is no one with the precise set of leadership qualities needed at this juncture. Contrary to conventional wisdom, it's not necessary for an organization to have an internal, homegrown heir apparent. In fact, some organizations benefit from an injection of new blood, fresh perspectives, and outside-the-box thinking. What is essential is that the organization has a capable team of senior managers who can provide sure-handed direction to the organization while the board searches for a new executive director.

Be sure that a strong board is in place.

The withdrawing executive director must make sure the organization has strong board leadership in place as well. At the very least, it needs to have a high-powered board chair who can lead the search process and catalyze the board into playing an active, robust role in ensuring the organization's continuity. Better yet, the executive director should invest as much in building the board as in developing the senior management team. The board should be highly engaged, responsible, and able to fill any gaps that arise during the transition—for example, raising funds, reassuring the staff, and maintaining key external relationships.

Systematically transfer the founding executive director's knowledge and relationships.

Plan on a generous transition period, during which the retiring executive director transfers to staff members his wealth of knowledge, important relationships, and valuable outside connections. During this transition period, the parting executive director should make sure that the organization's mission and core values are thoroughly understood and embraced by the staff and board so that he knows the fundamental character of the organization will be sustained after he's gone. Certainty that his legacy will be preserved is often the key to enabling the director to separate gracefully and without undue angst.

Refrain from putting the departing executive director on the board.

The exiting executive director usually should not be put on the board of directors. It's unfair and potentially stultifying to saddle the new executive director with a predecessor who's continuously looking over her shoulder and making invidious comparisons to "the way it's always been." Perhaps some years after the reins of leadership are securely in the hands of the new executive director, the former executive director can be safely given a seat on the board, but not until then.

Counter-Tensions to Manage

The organization fails to prepare and risks panic.

If the organization fails to prepare, it's normally knocked into a state of panic when the longtime executive suddenly announces his retirement or is forced to leave because of some incapacity. To avoid crisis, the board and senior managers must collect themselves and form a board-staff transition committee and enumerate steps to make the transition orderly, smooth, and free of trauma. The first thing they should do is retain a consultant or search firm to assess the kind of leader the organization now needs, help to find and recruit candidates, and manage the search process. The best cure for the anxiety and distressing sense of uncertainty that usually grips staff members when they learn their cherished leader will be leaving is to install a new executive director as quickly as possible.

It's time, but the longtime executive director won't leave.

Sometimes the long-tenured leader can't bear the thought of leaving and refuses to take any steps toward a leadership transition. He hangs on even though his vision and vigor are waning. Staff and board members begin to worry that he has become stale or complacent or lost his edge. They suspect that he's stayed too long, but no one wants to raise this with him for fear of hurting his feelings, or invalidating his past contributions, or appearing disloyal and ungrateful for his many years of service. They stick it out until it becomes clear that he and the organization are at a standstill, stuck in their ways, not adapting to new trends, and unable to meet the challenges created by a changed or volatile external environment. At this point, the board must step in and ease the director out to protect the organization from institutional inertia or ossification.

Helping a fading yet still well-liked executive director leave is a delicate task that must be executed with a combination of firmness, appreciation, sensitivity, and compassion. The staff and board must make sure that the director is fully thanked and acknowledged for all he's done so that he can leave with a sense of fulfillment and completion.

Staff experiences loss and insecurity.

If the executive director has remained a strong, vibrant, esteemed leader, his staff, particularly those who have worked with him for years, almost always experience a deep sense of loss about his pending departure. They're so used to being rewarded and affirmed by the executive director's approval that they don't know where their reinforcement will now come from. They feel unsettled and insecure. They worry that funding will dry up, that programs will stall, that they won't like the new director, or that he won't like them. They need to meet to express their grief and fears and to discuss the new possibilities and opportunities that will open up as the organization moves into this new era.

The longtime executive director sees he must leave but has more to contribute.

Sometimes a longtime executive director is still highly regarded by his staff and board, but even though they don't notice it, he knows that he's lost his entrepreneurial energy. He sees that the organization needs to move to the next level of effectiveness but recognizes that he's not the one to take it there. He knows that he should step down and make way for reinvigorated leadership, only he's not ready to retire. He thinks that he still has a contribution to make to the organization and would like to stay in some new, limited capacity, but all the books on management say that the old director absolutely must leave when the new one comes in.

Our experience has shown that under certain conditions, the former leader can stay as a staff member. First and most important, he must have an excellent relationship with the new director, one marked by openness, candor, mutual respect, and trust. This is most likely to occur if the new leader comes from inside the organization. Second, he must scrupulously avoid second-guessing or undermining the new executive director, never giving advice unless asked, and always relating to fellow staff members as a colleague, not a supervisor. Third, he must have a well-defined role with clear-cut boundaries. Fourth, not only must he stay off the board, but the board of directors should monitor the relationship between him and the new director and step in—or even ask him to leave—if serious tensions arise. Fifth, it's usually beneficial for the outgoing executive director to take a sabbatical for several months in order to give the new executive director time to establish her leadership. Finally, the former executive director must have the emotional strength to deal with the upsetting, unavoidable sense of dislocation he'll feel because of his loss of centrality and importance in the organization.

Turning Point 7: How Do We Move On?

Signs that change is needed

- The executive director has been with the organization for years, even decades.
- He is the lead visionary, strategist, spokesperson, and fundraiser, and no one else on staff can fill in.
- No one can imagine what the organization would be like without the executive director.
- Some fear the organization could not survive the executive director's departure.
- People think about succession planning, but keep their thoughts to themselves.
- The executive director has also thought about his departure, but worries about its impact on the organization.
- It suddenly is obvious that the executive will need to go: He or she is past retirement, is ill, or raises the issue.

Adjustments needed

- Prepare for a succession through an orderly process.
- Build a broad base of leadership.
- The new director doesn't have to be homegrown.
- Be sure that a strong board is in place.
- Systematically transfer the founding executive's knowledge and relationships.
- Refrain from putting the departing executive director on the board.

Counter-Tensions to Manage

- The organization fails to prepare and risks panic.
- It's time, but the longtime executive director won't leave.
- Staff experiences loss and insecurity.
- The longtime executive director sees he must leave but has more to contribute.

Rebalancing creative tensions

As shown in the figure below, the primary creative tensions to be rebalanced at this turning point are those related to management, decision-making, and governance.

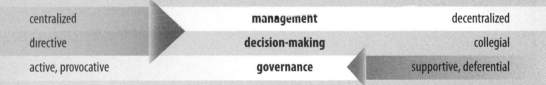

centralized	**management**	decentralized
directive	**decision-making**	collegial
active, provocative	**governance**	supportive, deferential

The change process needs to start by having the entire staff discover and understand the ways in which the organization's current structure is not working and the problem this creates.

How Do You Make Change Happen?

Change won't occur unless someone serves as a catalyst. This catalyst can be the executive director, a board or staff member, or even a funder. The process used to introduce change is as critical as the content.

SO, NOW THAT YOU KNOW the changes your organization needs to make because of the turning point (or points) it has reached, you're probably wondering: How do we make change happen?

Change won't occur unless someone serves as a catalyst, pointing out the need for change and getting the process started. The method by which the notion of change is introduced to the executive director and staff (and sometimes the board as well) can determine how quickly and easily they accept the need to change and how well they're prepared to handle the uncertainty, stress, and adjustment that change nearly always entails.

Getting an Executive Director to Change

At practically every turning point, executive directors have to transform themselves and adapt to their organizations' new circumstances. In order for their organizations to become stronger, sounder, and more effective, directors often need to change their management styles, their behaviors, their attitudes, and even the ways they think and what they place the greatest value on.

Unfortunately, most executive directors are unlikely to change, or even see the need for change, unless someone whom they listen to and respect makes them aware of the problems they're causing. Too often, an executive director stays stuck in counterproductive ways of operating simply because no one in the organization has been willing to face the discomfort and risk of pointing out problematic behaviors to her. If everyone in the organization waits to feel "comfortable" or "safe" before confronting the director, they will probably wait forever. Some brave soul—a trusted staff member, board member, or consultant—must speak up and serve as the change agent.

> If everyone in the organization waits to feel "comfortable" or "safe" before confronting the director, they will probably wait forever. Some brave soul—a trusted staff member, board member, or consultant—must speak up and serve as the change agent.

The change agent needs to start the conversation by putting the need for transformation into context. The director has to understand that while her methods were right for the organization at an earlier stage and propelled the organization to where it is today, the organization has arrived at a new level of development. The organization now requires a different kind of leadership, not because of a personal failing on the part of the director but rather because of the turning point the organization has reached. The change agent also needs to affirm the executive director's ways of leading and managing that continue to work and must be preserved, so that the baby is not thrown out with the bathwater. Most executives resist facing their weaknesses if they're not first acknowledged for their strengths.

Finally and most important, the change agent must point out the adverse impact the executive director's behavior, attitudes, and management/leadership style is having on her organization's maturation and effectiveness. Because of their deep commitment to their organizations' mission and goals, most executive directors are appalled to learn that some of their ways of operating and thinking are now working against their organizations' success. Nothing more powerfully induces executive directors to change than realizing that their vision for their organizations will probably not be realized unless they transform the way they think and operate to fit the turning point their organizations have reached.

To successfully navigate the change process, some executive directors may be helped by getting the support and guidance of an executive coach who can provide an executive director with useful insights, honest feedback, clear-eyed perspectives, and experienced advice.

Making Structural Change

Few things create more apprehension, anxiety, and upset in organizations than the prospect of structural change. Structural change includes redefining staff roles and responsibilities, changing who reports to whom, reorganizing staff into new units or departments, eliminating programs, or inserting a new layer of management between staff and the executive director.

At the end of the day, when structural changes have been implemented and adjusted to, they usually earn the staff's support because of the greater clarity and logic they've brought. Staff members find that they're more certain about what their jobs are, what their colleagues do, who reports to whom, and who is responsible for what. Managers find that they're much clearer about which people they're expected to supervise, the functions they're responsible for, the work other managers are in charge of, and who makes what decisions. Everyone finds that the organization's departments or work units are better delineated, more coherently and logically designed, and more conducive to supporting teamwork, synergy, and staff cohesion.

Structural change is essential at five of the seven turning points:

- ▸ *Turning Point 1: Do We Need to Get Organized?*
- ▸ *Turning Point 2: Do We Need Infrastructure?*
- ▸ *Turning Point 4: Do We Need Focus?*
- ▸ *Turning Point 5: Do We Need to Decentralize Power?*
- ▸ *Turning Point 6: Do We Need to Recapture Our Core?*

It's therefore almost inevitable that an organization, at some point, will have to restructure its management or reorganize its staff.

So the question becomes this: How does an organization manage the process of making structural changes in a way that creates as little apprehension, anxiety, and upset as possible? The process described below has stood the test of time. (Note that this process is basically the same process organizations should use in making significant changes in organizational policy or widespread practices.)

The process needs to start by having the entire staff discover and understand the ways in which the organization's current structure is not working and the problems this creates. For example, in a growing organization that is still trying to operate as a family, the staff might see that too many people report to the executive director. Everyone's work has become bottlenecked, awaiting her sign-off, and no one is getting as much direction, support, and guidance as he or she needs. Or, in an organization that is fragmented and has lost its core, the staff might see that the "siloing" of operations has blocked coordination, integration, and cross-fertilization among the staff.

An organization can, on its own, identify the flaws in its structure and the problems they cause by holding a lengthy meeting or retreat at which the executive director, managers, and staff examine together what's working and what's not about the structure. Some organizations prefer to retain a consultant to analyze their structure; his or her report then becomes the starting point for the discussion. In any case, the meeting should aim at six outcomes. Management and staff should

1. Identify the aspects of the structure that work well and should be preserved. (This reduces resistance to facing up to the aspects that need to change.)
2. Reach a common understanding of the deficiencies of the current structure and the problems they create.
3. Buy into the need to correct these problems and make the necessary structural changes.
4. Translate these problems into a set of goals the restructuring should achieve and endorse these goals as the rationale for and basis upon which any structural changes will be made.
5. Voice any fears or concerns people have about the prospect of change and brainstorm ideas about what the changes might be.
6. Turn over to the executive director and senior managers the difficult and sensitive task of designing the structural changes needed to reach the agreed-upon goals.

Once the executive director and senior leaders have completed developing their restructuring recommendations, they need to vet the proposed changes with the staff. Each senior manager may need to start the vetting process by meeting individually with members of their staff who will be most affected by the changes, explaining why the changes are necessary, and inviting reactions to them. These people may need to sit with this information for a day or two, so the senior manager has to be available to talk with them again.

Next, the organization's senior leadership, as a group, needs to meet with the whole staff (or whole departments in larger organizations) to present the proposed changes, explain why and how they will fulfill the restructuring goals, and ask for comments, concerns, and suggestions. In reviewing their recommendations with the staff, the senior managers have to emphasize that, while they're open to considering any adjustments or counterproposals the staff has to offer, they may end up not adopting the staff's suggestions, in which case they'll get back to the staff with the reasons why.

Even after all this groundwork, some members of the staff will be upset about the managers' recommendations because of the impact the changes will have on them. The senior managers will be able to depersonalize the situation by pointing to the agreed-upon restructuring goals and asking staff members to use these goals, instead of their feelings, as the measures against which to evaluate the wisdom of the proposed changes. The senior managers ought to strive to win broad staff support for the structural changes but not expect unanimity, because it's rarely achieved.

Some organizations make the mistake of trying to involve the whole staff in coming up with a specific restructuring design. This hardly ever works because it's hard for staff members to be objective about the structure and separate their own interests and needs from those of the institution. The process bogs down because too many strongly invested people are looking for solutions they'll all like, and they can't find them. In fact, sometimes senior managers themselves can't agree on answers to restructuring questions because their own feelings, interests, and preferences have gotten into the mix, so the executive director has to break the stalemate by making the decision.

It often pays to engage a consultant to guide the organization through the restructuring process. The consultant can avoid getting tangled up in everyone's vested interests and personal preferences and offer an objective, fresh, and informed perspective. A consultant who understands the organization's work and has experience in designing structures for organizations with similar goals and strategies will often see flaws that the organization is blind to. Because it's so hard for an organization to think outside its current structure, a consultant can come up with creative changes that the organization would never conceive of on its own. A consultant can also help an organization sort out whether a problem is rooted in the organization's structure or in the behavior of a particular person. Too many organizations step into the pitfall of trying to address personnel problems with structural solutions, and it almost never works.

Shifting an Organization's Culture

Every organization has a distinct culture that consists of the prevailing norms, values, assumptions, and beliefs that shape patterns of behavior and ways of thinking. Some common beliefs in nonprofit organizations are "everyone should be involved in everything," "avoid conflict," "it's unfair to fire people," or "keep everybody happy."

At five of the seven turning points, changing the organization's culture is an essential part of making the needed transition:

▸ When an organization reaches the point where it must get organized (*Turning Point 1*), it needs to give up its attachment to a loose, informal, familial way of operating and discover the benefits of more structure, definition, and specialization.

▸ When an organization reaches the point where it must develop its infrastructure (*Turning Point 2*), it needs to shift from caring only about programs to valuing management, infrastructure, and institutional development.

▸ When an organization reaches the point where it must focus (*Turning Point 4*), it needs to see that the rewards of operating with focus and discipline are greater than the rewards of operating as freewheeling, unbounded individual entrepreneurs.

▸ When an organization reaches the point where it must recapture its core (*Turning Point 6*), it needs to give up its attachment to operating autonomously as independent, self-defined projects and recognize the greater impact and value in having the organization function as one interconnected team whose members are focused on the same clear mission and shared, overarching goals.

▸ When an organization reaches the point where its longtime executive director must prepare to move on (*Turning Point 7*), the staff and board need to own up to their comfort in depending on the executive director, let go of their belief that the organization can't be as effective without her, and step up to their responsibility for ensuring its continued success.

No matter how its culture needs to shift, your organization requires the same basic group process. However, the players in the group process vary with the specific turning point: the executive director and staff alone, the board alone, the staff alone, or the executive director, staff, and board all together. In any case, there must be a leadership group that takes responsibility for the culture change process and has both the power and will to execute the necessary shifts. The process works best when facilitated by an outside consultant who understands the nature of the cultural shift that needs to be made. The process includes the following key elements:

- ► Reaffirming the aspects of the organization's culture that are working and should be preserved

- ► Confronting and owning up to the aspects of the organization's culture that are no longer working

- ► Uncovering the prevailing norms, values, assumptions, and beliefs that are shaping these unproductive behaviors and ways of thinking

- ► Admitting any attachment group members have to these patterns and acknowledging any ambivalence, fears, or sense of loss they have about giving them up

- ► Recognizing the negative impact these patterns of thinking and behaving are having on the organization's health and effectiveness

- ► Exploring the benefits to be gained and the new possibilities that will open up by breaking out of these patterns

- ► Identifying the behavioral and attitudinal changes that need to be made (by the executive director, senior managers, staff, or board) to shift the culture

- ► Identifying the policies and practices that are expressions of the old culture and need change

- ► Committing to making these changes in behavior, attitudes, policies, and practices and then following up with regular check-in meetings to make sure that the changes and culture shift are actually occurring

The Board's Role in Change

The board of directors can play a pivotal and even unique role in catalyzing the process of change at five of the seven turning points. Board action can be crucial:

▸ At *Turning Point 2: Do We Need to Get Organized?* when an organization's management needs outstrip the executive director's interests or skills.

▸ At *Turning Point 4: Do We Need Focus?* when an organization lacks focus and priorities and is spread too thin.

▸ At *Turning Point 5: Do We Need to Decentralize Power?* when an organization's growth is being thwarted by a domineering executive director.

▸ At *Turning Point 6: Do We Need to Recapture Our Core?* when an organization has fragmented and lost its core.

▸ At *Turning Point 7: How Do We Move On?* when an organization must prepare for a long-time leader to step down.

Whether the board of directors steps up to the challenge at these turning points depends in large measure on how seriously board members take their fiduciary responsibility for the organization. (To serve as a *fiduciary* means to hold something in trust.)

There are three fundamental ways in which a nonprofit board of directors is expected to fulfill this trusteeship: ensuring that (1) the organization's mission and goals are clear and being advanced, (2) the organization is financially sound, and (3) the organization is managed effectively.

First, the board is expected to ensure that the organization has a clear mission and central long-range goals and is focusing on the activities most important to achieving them. The board that embraces this responsibility insists on understanding all the organization's activities so it can assess how strategic and focused they are and how effectively they're advancing the organization's mission and goals. Because board members aren't immersed in the day-to-day activities of an organization, they can keep their eyes on the big picture and are in a far better position than the staff to detect signs that an organization has reached a turning point and needs to make systemic change. Boards can sense that an organization is going in too many directions, stretching its staff and resources too thin, or spot that an organization has splintered into separate projects with no coherence or overarching goals. By asking hard questions and serving as supportive but tough, honest critics, board members can push an organization to recapture its core, define its focus and priorities, consolidate its activities, and target its resources accordingly. And board members can stop an organization from taking on too much or going off on tangents.

The leaders and staffs of nonprofits, especially those working for social change, see so many unaddressed societal issues and problems that they often feel under enormous pressure to take on more than they can handle. A strong board saves the organization's executive director and staff from themselves—and ensures that the organization is making the most difference—by insisting that the executive director and staff identify the activities that are core and essential and then mandating and giving the executive director and staff permission to say "no" to everything else.

Second, the board, as the organization's fiduciary, is expected to safeguard the financial soundness and integrity of the organization and ensure that it has adequate resources and a stable, diverse funding base. When board members own this responsibility, they scrutinize budgets, audits, and quarterly financial reports; they demand to see the auditor's management letter; they ask the executive director probing questions about the organization's cash flow, financial reserves, and fundraising activities; and they don't tolerate getting board materials the day of their meeting. Taking these duties to heart enables the board to spot signs that the executive director is not paying enough attention to the organization's infrastructure and emboldens the board to insist that the executive make fundraising and financial management a much higher priority.

Third, the board of directors is expected to make sure that the organization is well led and well managed. The board must accept its unique responsibility for holding the executive director to account and calling her on counterproductive conduct. It should never fail to evaluate the executive director each year, be generous in its praise and rigorous in its criticism, demand improvement in substandard performance, and monitor growth and progress. When it is in the best interests of the organization, the board must accept the discomfort of asking the director to resign.

Sometimes the only way an organization can move successfully through a turning point is for the executive director to leave. This is nearly always the case when the time nears for a long-standing executive director to step down, often the case when an executive director is too controlling, frequently the case when a director is too weak to reintegrate a disjointed organization, sometimes the case when an executive director will not focus on anything but programming, and at times the case when an executive director won't provide any overall focus at all. When new leadership is needed, the board of directors is in the best and perhaps only position to make it happen.

What Funders Can Do

Organizations tend to hear suggestions from funders as conditions for getting grants. So while funders, whether foundation program officers, individual donors, or venture philanthropists, can often make the difference in whether organizations confront the changes they need to make at these turning points and negotiate them successfully, funders must be cautious about how they approach this role.

Sometimes funders are in a position to see the need for organizational change before the organization itself recognizes the need. For example, funders can see when an organization is going in so many different directions that there's no discernible overall mission or core (*Turning Point 6*). And they can see when a founding executive director has become so central and dominant that the organization could not function without her (*Turning Point 5*). In cases like these, funders can serve as catalysts for change, *but only if they're gentle and circumspect in the way they do it.*

Unless an organization truly feels that change is needed and voluntarily embraces it, the change will never take firm root and the organization is likely to drift back into old ways. One effective way for funders to encourage organizations to look at the need for change is by raising questions. For example, a funder can ask an unfocused organization these questions: Are there common goals that all your organization's work is aimed at achieving? What connects all your activities and makes them a coherent whole? Or a funder can ask an overbearing executive director: Who is on your senior management team and what role, responsibility, and authority does each senior manager have? What is your succession plan?

Funders also can make or break an organization's ability to get to the other side of these turning points by how willing they are to provide special, organizational development funding. Capacity-building grants, strategic planning grants, transition grants, or general support grants are crucial at many turning points:

▶ When an organization needs to expand its infrastructure and strengthen its management (*Turning Point 2*), it needs a capacity-building or general support grant.

▶ When a board-run organization needs to let go and hire its first staff (*Turning Point 3*), general support is essential.

▶ When an organization needs to focus (*Turning Point 4*), it first needs strategic planning grants and then broad program support or general operating support to implement its integrated, strategically targeted program.

▶ When an organizations needs to decentralize power (*Turning Point 5*), it needs capacity-building funding or general operating support to expand its senior management structure.

▶ When an organization needs to recapture its core (*Turning Point 6*), it needs a grant to conduct strategic planning and then a capacity-building grant to redesign its structure, build up its core program staff, and strengthen its central management.

▶ When an organization needs to move on and prepare for a longtime executive director's departure (*Turning Point 7*), it needs transition grants to broaden its base of leadership, engage in a systematic transfer of knowledge and relationships, and make other preparations for the longtime executive director to step down.

If a funder does provide funding for organizational development, it is critical that (1) the grantee chooses its own consultant, (2) the consultant reports to the organization, not the funder, and (3) the funder recognizes that change can be a long, rocky process with two steps forward and one step back. These conditions ensure that there's honesty and trust between the organization and the consultant and that the organization authentically owns the change process and actually implements the changes the consultant recommends.

Sometimes funders are so focused on programs that they fail to examine whether there's enough underlying organizational muscle. Like their grantees, funders need to appreciate how critical a strong, durable institutional foundation is to an organization's ability to persevere for the long haul and achieve its goals for society.

There are no permanent fixes for keeping an organization strong. You can, however, learn to see the signs when change is needed and strike the right balance between creative tensions.

General Principles for All Seven Turning Points

No matter which point—or combination of points—your organization is at or approaching, and no matter which of these transitions it is making, there are a few general principles that apply across the board.

There are no permanent fixes.

Unless an organization remains absolutely static, there are no lasting solutions, no permanent fixes. What worked at one stage eventually will not work at another.

Learn to recognize the signs of change as early as possible.

When an organization recognizes the symptoms signaling the need for change early in the cycle, it has more time to make the necessary adjustments. Thus, it should be able to avoid some of the stress, dislocation, and pain we've seen other organizations go through.

Strike the right balance between creative tensions.

There are always creative tensions involved in navigating the seven turning points. In moving through them, you'll have to find the right balance between:

1. Productive, efficient work environment versus nurturing, relational work environment.
2. Centralized management versus decentralized management.
3. Systematic operating style versus informal operating style.
4. Tight, integrated structure versus loose, mutable structure.
5. Directive decision-making versus collegial decision-making.
6. Well-defined, specialized staff roles versus fluid, adaptable staff roles.

7. Strategically planned program development versus opportunistic program development.

8. Institutional teamwork as standard for reward versus individual entrepreneurialism as standard for reward.

9. Active, provocative board governance versus supportive, deferential board governance.

10. Complex, highly developed infrastructure and systems versus simple, barebones infrastructure and systems.

11. Explicit, enforced personnel/operating rules versus implicit, flexible personnel/operating rules.

Take care when correcting an organization's undue tilt in one direction not to tilt too far in the opposite direction.

Don't personalize problems.

It's important to contextualize stresses and strains not as evidence that someone is a terrible manager, or that he has a lousy staff, but rather as the inevitable consequences of growth and other changes in the organization's internal and external environments. See them as symptoms that your organization's current structure and operating style no longer fit its circumstances, so it needs to make adjustments. Don't personalize this; that just creates defensiveness and pushback, compounds the tensions, and diverts attention from their real source.

Give it time.

Be patient. Change takes time. It is simply not possible for any organization to transform in a few weeks from an informal family style to a more tightly structured operation, or from a fragmented organization to a coherent, unified one. It takes months, sometimes a few years, to change not just structures but attitudes, habits, practices, and culture.

Make midcourse corrections.

Because of the counter-tensions that inevitably emerge, and because it's so hard to get every change absolutely right, the organization must be open and flexible, revisit or fine-tune changes, and make midcourse corrections.

Good change processes can help people adapt.

Good change processes are crucial. How changes are made is often as significant as what changes are made. The processes must ease people along with the change, emphasizing lots of communication, dialogue, explanation, and opportunities for input. The entire staff does not have to be thrilled, but a critical mass needs to buy in. Expect some inevitable resistance and discomfort. If the organization tries to wait for unanimous support before making changes, it's liable to wait forever.

Someone must catalyze the change.

Finally, change will generally not occur until somebody serves as a catalyst, flagging the need for change and tenaciously pushing for it. It can be the executive director, other key staff members, the board, an outside consultant, or sometimes even a funder who sparks the transition process.

Perfect, permanent equilibrium will never be reached by an organization. Nevertheless, periodically adjusting leadership, management, and other factors can help you achieve your goals to improve the world.

Afterword:
A Perpetual Balancing Act

AS YOU'VE SEEN while exploring the seven turning points, organizations never reach a point of perfect, permanent equilibrium. They must periodically adjust their leadership, structure, management, governance, and operating style to fit their changed circumstances if they are to move to new levels of effectiveness, impact, and staying power. Moreover, in navigating these turning points and dealing with the inevitable fallout from transitions, organizations must continually balance the creative tensions that are a natural part of organizational life. Examples of these tensions are the tension between being directive and being collegial, the push and pull between centralizing and decentralizing, or the tug between tight definition and fluid informality.

There are no right or wrong answers in this balancing act. There are only questions that an organization must continually ask itself: In what directions must our organization move to motivate, empower, and fulfill its people? How can we draw strength from our staff diversity? What must we do to have an active, contributing board? To have a staff that performs with excellence and accountability? To have a structure that supports and advances our programs? How can we be more strategic and intelligent in our decision-making? And, most of all, how can we make real our vision and achieve our goals for a better world?

Bibliography

Books

Bridges, William. *Managing Transitions: Making the Most of Change,* 2nd ed. Cambridge, MA: Perseus Publications, 2003.

Bryan, Barry. *Strategic Planning Workbook for Nonprofit Organizations,* revised and updated. St. Paul, MN: Amherst H. Wilder Foundation, 1997.

Carver, John. *Boards That Make a Difference,* 3rd ed. San Francisco: Jossey-Bass, 2006.

Houle, Cyril O. *Governing Boards.* San Francisco: Jossey-Bass, 1989.

Klein, Kim. *Fundraising for Social Change,* 5th ed., revised and expanded. San Francisco: Jossey-Bass, a Wiley Imprint, 2007.

———. *Fundraising for the Long Haul.* San Francisco: Jossey-Bass, 2000.

Schein, Edgar H. *Organizational Culture and Leadership.* San Francisco: Jossey-Bass, 2004.

Senge, Peter M. *The Fifth Discipline.* New York: Currency/Doubleday, 2006.

Articles and Booklets

Advancing Your Cause Through the People You Manage. Washington, DC: Management Assistance Group, 2007.

Boards Matter. Washington, DC: Management Assistance Group, 2007.

Collins, James C., and Jerry Porras. "Building Your Company's Vision." *Harvard Business Review,* September-October 1996.

Collins, Jim, and William Lazier. "Is This Any Way to Run a Business?" *Stanford Business School Magazine,* June 1991.

Fram, Eugene H., and Robert F. Pearse. "When Worse Comes to Worst: Terminating the Executive Director." *Nonprofit World,* volume 8, no. 6.

Fry, Ronald. "Accountability in Organizational Life." *Nonprofit Leadership and Management,* Winter 1995.

Gabarro, John J., and John P. Kotter. "Managing Your Boss." *Harvard Business Review,* January-February 1980.

Galford, Robert, and Anne Seibold Drapeau. "The Enemies of Trust." *Harvard Business Review,* 2003.

Gilmore, Thomas N. *Finding and Retaining Your Next Chief Executive: Making the Transition Work.* Washington, DC: Board Source, 1993.

Goffee, Robert, and Gareth Jones. "Why Should Anyone Be Led by You?" *Harvard Business Review,* September-October 2000.

Grant, Heather McLeod, and Leslie R. Crutchfield. "Creating High Impact Nonprofits." *Stanford Innovation Review,* Fall 2007.

Greiner, Larry E. "Evolution and Revolution as Organizations Grow." *Harvard Business Review,* May 1, 1998.

Kotter, John. "Leading Change: Why Transformation Efforts Fail." *Harvard Business Review,* March-April, 1995.

Lauenstein, Milton C. "Preserving the Impotence of the Board." *Harvard Business Review,* July-August, 1977.

Light, Paul. "The Spiral of Sustainable Excellence." *Nonprofit Quarterly,* January 14, 2008.

Mathiasen, Karl. *Board Passages: Three Key Stages in a Nonprofit Board's Life Cycle.* Washington, DC: Board Source, 1990.

"Race Matters Toolkit," web-based collection of publications. Baltimore, MD: Annie E. Casey Foundation, 2005, racematters@aecf.org.

Rangan, V. Kasturi. "Lofty Mission, Down-to-Earth Plans." *Harvard Business Review,* March 2004.

Redington, Emily, and Donn Vickers. *Following the Leader: A Guide for Planning Founding Executive Director Transition.* Academy for Leadership and Governance, 2001.

Strategic Planning that Makes a Difference. Washington, DC: Management Assistance Group, 2007.

Index

More Results-Oriented Resources from Fieldstone Alliance

Practical books are just one of the resources Fieldstone Alliance has to offer. We also provide consulting, training, and demonstration projects that help nonprofits, funders, networks, and communities achieve greater impact.

As a nonprofit ourselves, we know the challenges that you face. In all our services, we draw on our extensive experience to provide solutions that work:

EXPERT CONSULTATION

Our staff and network of affiliated consultants are recognized nonprofit leaders, authors, and experts with deep experience in managing organizations, teaching, training, conducting research, and leading community initiatives. We provide assessment, planning, financial strategy, collaboration, and capacity-building services. Contracts range from short-term assessments to the management of multi-year initiatives.

PROVEN TRAINING

Training can be a powerful change strategy when well designed. Our experienced staff, authors, and network of experts from across the United States provide practical, customized training for nonprofits, foundations, and consultants. From one-hour keynote addresses to multi-session programs, we offer expertise in various aspects of capacity building, nonprofit management, leadership, collaboration, and community development. Coupling training with books and follow-up support increases retention and application of what is learned.

DEMONSTRATION PROJECTS

Fieldstone Alliance conducts research and hosts demonstration projects that have promise for improving performance and results in the nonprofit sector. Through this work we mine best practices, package the findings into practical, easy-to-apply tools, and disseminate them throughout the sector.

To find out more, call 1-800-274-6024. Or visit www.FieldstoneAlliance.org.

▶ SEE MORE BOOKS AND FREE RESOURCES

Free Resources

GET FREE MANAGEMENT TIPS!

Sign-up for *Nonprofit Tools You Can Use,* Fieldstone Alliance's free e-newsletter. In each issue (arriving twice a month), we feature a free management tool or idea to help you and your nonprofit be more effective.

Content comes from our award-winning books, our consultant's direct experience, and from other experts in the field. Each issue focuses on a specific topic and includes practical actions for putting the information to use.

There are more than 70 great issues in the archive!

ONLINE RESOURCES

Here are other free resources you'll find on our web site:

Articles
In-depth information on key nonprofit management issues.

Assessment Tools
See how your organization or collaboration is doing relative to characteristics of a successful nonprofit.

Research Reports
See research that was done to inform our demonstration projects and consulting practice.

Related Books

The Nonprofit Strategy Revolution
Real-Time Strategic Planning in a Rapid-Response World

This ground-breaking guide offers a compelling alternative to traditional strategic planning. You'll find new ideas for how to form strategies, and the tools and framework needed to infuse strategic thinking throughout your organization. The result: your nonprofit will be more strategic in thought and action on a daily basis. When the next opportunity (or challenge) comes along, you'll be able to respond swiftly and thoughtfully.

by David La Piana | 208 pp | 2008 | ISBN 978-0-940069-65-7 | order no. 069657

Generations
The Challenge of a Lifetime for Your Nonprofit

What happens when a management team of all Baby Boomers leaves within a five year stretch? Peter Brinckerhoff tells you what generational changes to expect and how to plan for them. You'll find in-depth information for each area of your organization—staff, board, volunteers, clients, marketing, technology, and finances.

by Peter Brinckerhoff | 232 pp | 2007 | ISBN 978-0-940069-55-8 | order no. 069555

Financial Leadership for Nonprofit Executives
Guiding Your Organization to Long-term Success

Provides executives with a practical guide to protecting and growing the assets of their organizations while accomplishing as much mission as possible with those resources.

by Jeanne Bell & Elizabeth Schaffer | 144 pp | 2005 | ISBN 978-0-940069-44-2 | order no. 06944X

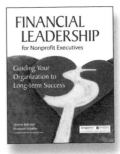

Benchmarking for Nonprofits
How to Measure, Manage, and Improve Results

This book defines a formal, systematic, and reliable way to benchmark (the on-going process of measuring your organization against leaders), from preparing your organization to measuring performance and implementing best practices.

by Jason Saul | 144 pp | 2004 | ISBN 978-0-940069-43-5 | order no. 069431

The Five Life Stages of Nonprofit Organizations
Where You Are, Where You're Going, & What to Expect When You Get There

Shows you what's "normal" for each development stage which helps you plan for transitions, stay on track, and avoid unnecessary struggles. Includes an assessment.

by Judith Sharken Simon with J. Terence Donovan
128 pp | 2001 | ISBN 978-0-940069-22-0 | order no. 069229

The Manager's Guide to Program Evaluation
Planning, Contracting, and Managing for Useful Results

Explains how to plan and manage an evaluation that will help identify your organization's successes, share information with key audiences, and improve services.

by Paul W. Mattessich, PhD | 112 pp | 2003 | ISBN 978-0-940069-38-1 | order no. 069385

Nonprofit Stewardship
A Better Way to Lead Your Mission-Based Organization

You may lead a nonprofit, but it's not your organization; it belongs to the community it serves. You are the steward—the manager of resources that belong to someone else. The stewardship model of leadership can help you make decisions that are best for the people you serve by keeping your mission foremost.

by Peter C. Brinckerhoff | 272 pp | 2004 | ISBN 978-0-940069-42-8 | order no. 069423

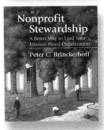

Strategic Planning Workbook, Revised and Updated

Chart a wise course for your nonprofit's future. This time-tested workbook gives you practical step-by-step guidance, real-life examples, and one nonprofit's complete strategic plan.

by Bryan W. Barry | 144 pp | 1997 | ISBN 978-0-940069-07-7 | order no. 069075